Hip Ho

"Fleetwood is one person that has had a long journey trying to find the treasures in Hip Hop and, in his days, became a writer, rap artist, music producer, videographer, motivational speaker and a community activist. With roots in both California and North Carolina, Fleetwood embodies the best of both sides of the coast. As much as he has a southern accent, he also has a lot of West Coast flavor.

Fleetwood loves working in the community with young people. He regularly volunteers for a youth program called Straight Forward Club.

Today, Fleetwood is a man of God never trying to be perfect but appreciative of his life and shares his experiences about his journey in hip hop with others in San Quentin Prison, juvenile hall facilities and youth programs across the Bay Area."

— Ben Bautista
Director of Straight Forward Boxing Club

"I have known Fleetwood for some years. We met when we was both in the game and running the streets. He was fucking with some of the young homeys from Hunters Point, on some rap shit. We use to run into each other all throughout the city streets and at all the get moneyspots. Fleetwood at that time was a wild ass nigga, on some gangster, shoot, gimme the loot type shit. That nigga been shot, stabbed hella times, he like a walking war wound-a soldier of the hood. He was a good dude then, even though he was intimidating looking-short black and baldheaded. Other mutherfuckers use to say, here come Fleetwood and run off the block, I never looked at him like that, real niggaz is my patnas. I seen him become a changed man. He still the realest he just doing it in a positive way."

— Kevin Epps
Filmmaker/producer

Hip Hop Tried
2
Kill Me

Hip Hop Tried

2

Kill Me

FLEETWOOD

2008 Uaintgettinmy Publishing
Oakland

Hip Hop Tried 2 Kill Me
Published in the United States by
Uaintgettinmy Publishing
634 - 15th Street, Suite 526
Oakland, CA 94612

First edition published 2008.

Adobe® and Chaparral® are either registered trademarks or trademarks
of Adobe Systems Incorporated in the United States and/or other
countries.

Cover Design: "Shadow Monk" of grafftrixx.com
Book Design: Paula Hendricks of Cinnabar Bridge and kwan Booth

ISBN: 978-0-9815932-0-3

This book is printed on acid-free paper.

THIS BOOK IS DEDICATED 2:

PIMP C
JAM MASTER JAY
MAUSBERG
FREAKY TAH
EAZY- E
PROOF
AALIAYAH
BIG PUN
JOHNNY CASH
LISA "LEFT EYE" LOPEZ
OLD DIRTY BASTARD
TROUBLE T ROY
SEAGRAM
COUGNUT
BIG MELLO
MR. C
HITMAN
MAC DRE
BIG L
J DILLA
MAXACIOUS
SOULJA SLIM
SWEET T
DJ SCREW
PROFESSOR X
NOTORIOUS BIG
TUPAC

AND LAST BUT NOT LEAST TO MY LITTLE SOLDIER
WHO NEVER MADE IT INTO THIS CORRUPT WORLD.
I'LL SEE YOU WHEN I GET HOME SON.
I LOVE YOU.

ACKNOWLEDGEMENTS

There's no way I could have written this book without the help and encouragement of some key people at crucial times. To them I say "thanks for helping me and being there though all the phases of this project First of all GOD my partna Kevin Weston, Paula Hendricks, Tony Coleman, Bubba Hamp, Marvelous Marv, Ben Bautista, Kwan Booth and Shadow Monk, who did all the graphics. And thanks to my homey GOD Supreme and the Champaign Kings for all their support and can't forget my family member who always come thru fo me, MR. MISTER, we winning with this one Mister and last but not least I wanna thank GOD my lord and Savior my big homey my friend and protector who gave me the gift of the holy spirit without him none of this would have been able to happen thank you JESUS praise his name, praise his name.

CHAPTER 1

I'm what you call a divorce toy. I was born in San Francisco, California. My dad was in the Air Force and moved his family out there from North Carolina. He traveled back to marry my moms and they returned to the West Coast.

At age three, my parents started arguing and eventually decided to split up. So my mother grabbed me and we moved back to North Carolina. I can't remember me and moms ever havin a conversation bout why her and my pops broke up, nor do I remember her bad mouthing my dad. I can't never remember her waitin on a child support check from him and I never really seen a photo wit them together either, I just knew I had family on both coasts. Between west and south, I must have attended over 20 schools, but Moms always made sure that I knew I was from California and just livin in North Carolina.

Right from the jump the first thing I noticed bout North Carolina was there was no water. No ocean, no bridges, no hills – it was just a whole lotta trees everywhere wit green grass and big back and front yards and all the houses were made of brick instead of stucco. At night the sound of crickets could be heard and you would see these lighting bugs flyin around that lit up like a bulb. I was amazed by that and use to love to catch those lighting bugs. All of this gave off a certain warmth: the feelin was different, even though it was dangerous still in certain places.

One thang that's unforgettable bout North Carolina is the presence of black colleges. This brought all kinds of events weekly to the towns and cities, like the annual home comings, where people from the past would comeback to celebrate their college experience.

See in the south, you could find black, educated, prosperous people everywhere and this made you as a youth feel like you could be something in life, and wit it's long sports tradition this was a breedin ground for athletes. Friday nights were big and everybody could be found at the local high schools watchin ball games just to see who was gonna be the next to make it to college to rep the city. The playgrounds stay packed wit youngstas perfectin their skills, waitin on their chance to become the next Michael Jordan, who was also in North Carolina at the time, somewhere on a ball court.

The projects were so different lookin but you could tell they were projects. They were one and two story buildings stuck together. Rows and rows of them that didn't blend into the fabric of the city at all. In California they really looked like apartments. The next thing I noticed was it was only two kinds of people: black and white. The Bay Area it was a meltin pot for different cultures: Filipino's, Chinese, Ghanian, Italian, Mexican, and the list goes on. I also noticed that all the local hustlas were posted in front of all the corna stores, grittin and grindin, where in California it was more in the hood or in the house.

I'll never forget hearing "Rappers Delight" on the radio that first mornin. It was my tenth grade year and there I was layin in my bed when all of a sudden I heard this voice comin out the speaker "hip hop, the hibbie to the hibbie... hip hip hoppin you don't stop rockin" ya'll know the rest.

I raised up on my elbows from under my covers and reached over and turned up the volume. At first I thought it was some kinda practical joke or maybe somebody had took over the radio station, drunk on some Wild Irish Rose. But the more I listened I realized this was something fresh, something new and at that point I knew I had to find some kind of way to be involved. This was what I wanted to do wit my life. I just had to find out how I was gonna be a part of it. Little did I know I would spend the next twenty years of my life chasin that feelin that I got when I first heard that song comin out of that speaker. I wanted so bad for it to be my voice, my song, feel me?

When rap emerged I thought it was a new, magic way of talkin. As I walked toward the bus stop the mornin I heard "Rapper's Delight" I could hear the discussion already in progress. I wasn't the only one who had heard the song that mornin.

"Man ya'll hear that new song on the radio this mornin? That was bad!"

One kid was like "My cousin from Harlem be singin like that when we go up there in the summer. I know how to a little bit."

When he broke off into his routine I was amazed. I thought you had to be from New York to rap, but by this time I was already into so much bullshit in school and the streets that I didn't get into the art of rap until later.

At 17 in 1979, my moms died. I can see it like yesterday.

I was sittin in the crib smokin some weed wit my partnas Cooley and Fred Smith. In walked my brotha – tall, lighter than me, kinda like a black hippie – we never really got along since we was little. He had left to visit momma in the hospital a few hours before and tried to get me to go wit him.

"Robert you need to go to the hospital. Your momma really sick."

"Man you know I don't like those damn places."

"Boy you need to go see your momma."

"Alright alright nigga, I'mma go. Damn." I never went.

I figured she'd come home like she always did. This time was different. As the door closed behind my brotha I could tell something was wrong from the look on his face. He didn't have the usual arrogance.

"Your momma gone boy. She died this mornin at 5:15. I told you to go over there but n'all, you'd rather be here smokin weed wit these niggaz."

"What you talkin bout momma dead?" My high went away real

quick.

'She's dead, she's gone. I told you to go see her."

"Man you lyin. For real?"

"Yeah for real boy. You need to put that damn weed out and clean this damn house up."

"Man quit tryin to tell me what to do. You always tryin to tell me what to do." Then he ran up on me and we got to chuckin. He was hurtin and I was the closest thing to the enemy. My homeys broke us up and I bailed. We went and got some more weed and beer then went and sat in the park. The sun was just comin up and it seemed like the rays of light was talkin to me, tryin to guide me somewhere but I couldn't understand where. After we finished the weed and beer my homeys said they had to go home.

"Rob you gonna be alright homey?"

"Yeah I'm cool."

"Soon as I change clothes and do my chores I'll be back down here."

"Yeah we'll be back in like a hour."

"Cool, if I ain't here I'll be at the crib."

Man I was lost and alone, I didn't know what to do. My best friend, my protector was gone for good. She wasn't comin home from the hospital this time.

My mother was the oldest girl in a family of seven: five girls and two boys. Right after high school and college my other aunties and uncles left North Carolina for big northern cities like New York, Philly and Washington DC but not my mother. She loved my grandmother Granny B and wasn't bout to leave her. They were best friends and I think this kinda had something to do wit my moms wantin to leave California whenever my pops did the least little thing wrong, never mind that other shit she discovered later. My moms was one of the sweetest human beings GOD ever created. One of his best angels. To this day I can honestly say I can't ever remember hearing her use profanity. She wasn't perfect, but damn near. I remember she kept her a bottle of Inver House liquor stashed away. I know. I usta sneak into it.

A lotta successful women and their daughters in the Greensboro, North Carolina community were influenced by my mother and they'll tell you that. I still remember all the young girls in the neighborhood comin over to my house, gettin their hair fixed, pressed and curled for free to get ready for Sunday church service. I also remember my mom teachin the young girls how to sew and makin all their cheerleading outfits when I was in the seventh grade. She didn't ask for nothin and to be honest, I usta get mad. I was feelin like they needed to go home to their own momma. That's my momma! I didn't like sharing her wit nobody, I was her baby! Eventually it made me realize how great she was.

See, not only was my mother a social worker at the welfare building but she was also a beautician and a seamstress. I still remember going to my mother's office and playin wit the food stamps in her drawer. I thought it was monopoly money. Later in life I'd discover what food stamps really was. My mother was strictly devoted to worshippin GOD. She was an usher, sang in the choir, and was basically involved in every aspect of the church. I remember several mornings wakin to the sound of James Cleveland and Shirley Ceaser blaring over the house stereo. I'd try to cover my ears wit my pillow but it always seeped in. I'm so thankful now that it did.

I usta tell her "momma can u turn that music down some!"

She'd say "boy this my house! You ain't payin no bills here. What you need to do is get up and get ready to go to church."

"I don't wanna go this week" I'd say.

"Well if you don't go you definitely ain't gonna play no basketball. When I get back you gonna stay in this house all day."

"Always put your faith in God son," my mother usta tell me. "Follow the ten commandments in the bible. It'll guide you through life. One day I won't be here to protect you and you gonna miss your momma when she's gone."

"Mama why u always say that. I don't want u to go nowhere I'mma be good, mama I promise I'mma be good."

I wasn't a bad kid really. I just had no one to discipline me. I would cuss teachers out, be like "I ain't trying to hear that shit" and the whole time I was gettin A's and B's in their classes so it would amaze them that I would snap. I remember I usta stay after school when they had teachers meetings and would creep into the teachers lodge and hit all their purses. The next day I would be smilin at they azz in school like "yeah I got that azz yesterday." It was just the fact of me gettin back at them, not the money, and them not knowin it was me that excited me, feel me?

Punk azz niggaz usta fuck wit me because I was always the new kid in school. I had cousins all over the city though and most of them was from the projects and not to be fucked wit. I was hella dark but I had a certain air to myself, boy I had a cold azz pimp walk, still do to this day. See, I knew I was somebody and them ho azz niggaz didn't like that, so they tried me. I got stole on one time and after that I was stealin on niggaz daily. I stayed in the assistant principal's office. At that time you could get three licks on the azz or get suspended. Shit I usta wear three pairs of extra gym shorts everyday! I knew I was gonna get three licks sooner or later before the day ended.

My moms worked so hard and she was rarely home. When she was, she was tired. On top of that she was always sick and was always in the hospital for one surgery or another. To this day I think that's why I can't stand them damn places. Bout the time I got to the seventh grade she had stopped whoopin me. She was like "baby, these streets will never love you, but GOD always will and I will always love you. But if you don't mind me, them white folks in that jail house gonna make you mind!"

By that time I had graduated to breakin in mutha fuckas houses and skippin school. It was just a thrill to break in someone house, sit there, eat their food, watch TV then ransack the joint. It was nuts! I can admit that shit when I think bout it now. I never imagined being in jail, but moms saw it comin. Just like everything else.

Imagine summer every day. That's California. The Southern life was cool, but it was too slow compared to the fast track I had seen in Cali when I was younger. As the months passed in North Carolina I stayed in trouble, stayed drunk, stayed high. One day I got a letter from an insurance company statin that I had an inheritance comin on my 18th birthday. I'd been receiving social security checks that would last until I was 18 and moms had left me and my brotha a house, but it was still money left to pay on it. I pretty much thought that was it. I'd never really tripped on an inheritance. When my birthday came I went to the insurance company and it was two checks waitin for me .

The first thing I did, like a dumbazz, was go out and buy a car – a 1977 Celica, burgundy wit gold and white strips. Rollin off the lot I headed straight to the rim shop to get some triple basket spoke rims wit knockoff's. At the time that was the shit. Then I went and got a sunroof put in, then a spoiler on the back of it, all in one day. After that I went to the car wash, shined it up and I was ready. In between stops I copped me a quarter pound of weed and a case of beer. It was my birthday nigga!

I was feelin like a million so I headed to the local hangout spot where all the playas use to hang. Monroe's was a carhop like on "Happy Days" where the waiters and waitress came to your car to take your order. Nigga I pulled in that joint and all heads turned and mouths dropped like "damn!"

I was goin hella slow so they could get a good look, wit that new Cameo bumpin "Shake your pants." I backed my car in the slot feelin like I was the shit. I must have smoked two ounces of weed that night.

I already had a '69 Torino my brotha had brought me to go to school wit like six months prior, but I couldn't wait to show off the new one. I hit every spot in the city and all people could say was "damn that's your ride? Where you get that at? How much that cost? Look at those rims!"

And you know the breezies was all like "Rob, can we ride wit you, wit your cute black self!" At that point, my game wasn't tight, so I usually told them all to get in. Every week I had a skip party at the house. We would close all the curtains, all the kids would skip school and come to the crib and we would do the fool!

At one party, this girl name Jewel asked me: "Rob, why you got all these people in your momma house like this? If this was my momma house I wouldn't have none of these niggaz up in here, tearing my momma house up she left for me to live in."

I told her "You know, you the first person ever said something like that to me."

"You need to think bout that. These niggaz don't care bout you they usin you."

"I appreciate you tellin me that, " I said. "If it's anything I can do for you, let me know."

"That's what I'm talkin bout! You need to concentrate on helpin yourself."

I looked at her and for the first time realized how I was disrespectin my mother's memory. It had been almost a year since my mother had died though and by that time I was full fledge wildin. One day I was takin my uncle home and this car came outta no where and we had a head on collision. The punk police said it was my fault and since I didn't have full coverage I had to pay for her car and mine. I had just had the car back from the shop for two weeks when one night, after droppin off my homeys Sevelie and Cudda Bug, I wrecked again. My car slid in the snow right into another car. I just sat there cryin. Not from pain but from what had happened. I thought it was bad luck but it was far from it.

By this time the mortgage was past due and the bank foreclosed on our house. My car was fucked up and I had no where to stay. I was homeless. My homeboy Sevelie was bout to do 3 to 5 years so he called his moms:

"Mom, can Rob stay in my room while I'm gone?"

She was like "Give him the phone."

"Rob, I ain't havin none of that mess in my house and if you can't go by my rules you can't live here."

I told her "yes ma'am."

Her name is Ms. Bobbie Ireland and to this day she's like my second mother. I'll always love her, but after stayin there awhile me and her brotha got into it and I left. I had started doin labor work for this construction company so I was cool on the money side. The boss owned a liquor house and he was like "look Rob, if you wanna, you can go live in the liquor house. Watch out for it and I wont charge you that much for rent."

My mother was buried in the cemetery across the street from the liquor house, where I'd be layin my head and sellin liquor every night, but I had nowhere else to go. It was all bad and fucked up for me. Every time I'd go out the door or look out the window it hurt.

One day I started writin what became my first song, "Better Days." That same night after I completed the song, I took all the earnins, grabbed my bags and headed to the Greyhound Bus Station. I just couldn't deal wit that shit no more, knowin how hard my moms had worked to provide a good life for me and here I was livin in a nasty azz liquor house sellin liquor across the street from were she was buried. At first I was like this the payback for how I disrespected her memory but then I realized she wouldn't want that for me so I was like "fuck this shit." I bounced. I knew it was better days ahead for me and I was gonna find them, feel me?

CHAPTER 2

At that time the south was the south and not much was goin on for young blacks. It was no gold crusted diamond grills and it definitely wasn't no crack to get fast money off of, just yellow envelopes of nickel bags of weed. The New York influence wasn't down there yet. For the lil' mamas it was no strips clubs to dance in and crunk music hadn't emerged yet. Niggaz was cool though but still, it was country. Go to college, work in a factory or you're fucked. I founded out there was a big construction job a few towns away and I really wanted to get away. I'd had enough and as I rode the Greyhound I looked through the glass window at the fields of tobacco. The bright green leaves and stalks of corn reminded me of when me and my grandmother would get up early to pick from the garden. I closed my watery eyes and made her and my momma a promise. I told them I was sorry for what I had did and that I was gonna make them proud of me.

I ended up in Winston Salem, NC. As the bus pulled into the station I didn't know what was waitin on me but I knew it was a new beginning. I'd got a number out the newspaper in Greensboro and had talked to a man who told me he would hire me. I just hoped he wasn't playin. I dialed and was hella nervous standing in that bus station waitin on someone to answer.

"Hello, Williams Precast Concrete."

"How you doin sir. This is Robert Bowden. I had spoke to you on the phone early this week."

"Oh yeah I remember you, you the young man who said he would travel anywhere for a good job."

"Yes sir. I'm here now in Winston ready to go to work."

"Where you at exactly?"

"I'm at the Greyhound bus station, sir."

"Do you have somewhere to stay?"

"No sir, not exactly."

"Call this number. It's a boardin house where all the guys stay at. Ask for Mr. Earl. Tell him Jesse Ray sent you and he'll put you up 'til you get paid."

"Thank you sir."

"No problem, just go there and get settled in. It's a few guys who work for me there. Come wit them to the site in the mornin."

"Thank you again. I'll see you in the mornin."

"Alright son."

"Good night."

I dialed the number Mr. Williams had given me.

"Hello."

"How you doin, sir? My name is Robert Bowden. Mr. Jesse Ray he told me to give you a call bout puttin me up until I get my first check."

"What did you say your name was?"

"Robert Bowden."

"Do you know where the house is?"

"No sir."

"Where are you right now?"

"The Greyhound bus station."

"Stay there. I'll have someone come and pick you up. Be standing out front."

"No problem. Thank you very much."

A black pick up truck pulled up within an hour.

"Is your name Robert Bowden" this white bearded dude asked out of his passenger window.

"Yeah."

"Well come on get in man, I'm Joel."

"How you doin?"

'I'm alright."

"So you just got into town?"

"Yeah."

"You ever did this kinda work before?"

"What, precast?"

"Yeah man."

"N'all, not really."

"Well it ain't nothin. If you fall it's only gonna hurt one time!"

He let out a loud laugh, but I didn't find that shit funny. Finally we made it to the boardin house and I got settled in. As the weeks passed I developed a routine: work, sleep, save money, and after six weeks the job was over.

It was 1981 and it was work all over the US. I was wit it because I was tryin to get as far away from Greensboro as possible. I saw a job in Clayton, New Mexico. I called and as the phone rang I stood there full of anticipation.

A lady answered. "B. Daniels Maintenance."

"Yes ma'am, my name is Robert Bowden. I'm callin from North Carolina and I was told y'all might have some work available."

"Hold on sir, let me let you speak to our labor foreman, Mike."

A man picked up. "Hello?"

"How you doin sir? I'm callin from North Carolina and I was wondering whether or not y'all had some work available."

"What kinda position are you lookin for son?"

"Well I'll do anything you need done."

"I tell you what. You get here and you got a job."

"Thank you sir. Thank you."

"Wait a minute, you didn't even ask how much the job was payin."

"Oh yeah, how much sir?"

"10 hours a day, $10 a hour. How bout that?"

"That sounds good to me."

"Okay how long will it take you to get here?"

"I should be there in a week."

"See ya when you get here Robert."

"Yes sir and thank you again." I stood there wit a Kool-Aid smile. I was on my way outta North Carolina to New Mexico! And back then $10 a hour was a lotta money.

The bus ride to New Mexico reminded me of an old John Wayne movie – goin across all those states and finally crossin Texas, lookin out the window at the tumble weeds rollin over, lookin at how flat Texas was – no hills or nothin. You could see straight for miles and miles and it was so hot you could see heat rays comin off the road. Finally we made it across Texas and entered New Mexico. The bus pulled into Clayton and as soon as I got off I could tell I was in cattle territory as the smell of horse shit flooded my nostrils immediately. Man I just knew I was in a cowboy movie then! It was one main street and I felt like I had went into a time capsule and ended up on the set of "Gun Smoke." All the store fronts were made of old wood material and it was a few cowgirls in tight azz jeans and boots walkin around lookin cute but I didn't holla. That's when white women still had flat azzes, not like today.

I saw a cowboy ride in on a horse, get off it and tie it up to a pole then go in the saloon wit swinging doors. I started laughin like "damn what the fuck I done got myself into?" That's when I realized, from the looks I got, that I was probably the only black person these people had ever seen in real life. Behind the main street were the most beautiful mountains I've ever seen in my life. It was like someone had went up there and took a paint brush and painted each mountain one at a time.

I found a hotel, got settled in and took a walk to the store. I noticed how people where staring, but they all were friendly so I didn't really trip. Finally, I found a bar and went inside. This big white boy who looked like a welder sat down beside me.

"How's it goin there buddy," he said in a thick Texas drawl.

"I'm cool, how you feelin man?"

"Ah hell you know, tryin to pay these dang bills to keep the old lady happy. Where you from?"

"I'm from California but I also grew up in North Carolina. I'm just comin from a job down there."

"Well hell, what made you come out here?"

"Work boss. I needed to work."

"So you at the site outside of town?"

"Yeah I hope that's the one. I called a man name Jesse Ray and he told me to come here. He was from B. Daniels Maintenance."

"Oh hell yeah! That's one of the biggest outfits in the Southwest. They out there. Listen, you in that hotel down the road right?"

"How you know?"

"Shit, that's the only one in town."

"You don't say. In this big city?"

"Yeah, this big city. Anyway, you want a lift to the job site in the mornin?"

"Man that would be cool. What time you pullin out?"

"Bout 5 AM."

"I'll be ready. What's your name big man?"

"They call me Tex. What bout you?"

"Call me Rob."

"Alright Rob. I'll see you in the mornin."

As he got up off the stool and walked away, the sound of a true Texan: cowboy boots slammin against a wood floor. I went there the next mornin, met Jesse Ray and everything was cool. I went right to work on a crew wit nothin but Mexicans. I can't lie, them cats work. Work for real. One young stocky guy spoke good English.

"Where you from Holmes" he said wit a hint of arrogance.

"I'm from California dude."

"Why you come down here?"

"Same reason you here" lettin him know he wasn't dealin wit no punk. He just stared at me for a moment.

"You know you the first black person to ever come to this town?"

"Yeah I kinda figured that."

"Well look Holmes, you drink beer?"

"Yeah."

"What bout mota?"

"What?"

"Mota you smoke mota"

"What's that?"

"Weed. You smoke weed?"

Now he was talkin. Hadn't hit no weed since I left North Carolina.

"Hell yeah, you got some?"

"I keep weed. Look, when we get off I'll come and pick you up and we'll go cruise."

"Cool homey, what's your name?"

"Lou. Lou Trujillo. What's your name?"

"Call me Rob."

"Man you look like Larry Holmes ay," and we all started laughin.

That night we must have rode up and down that one strip of road like 200 times, back and forth wit bout 20 other cars. This was the city's younger crowd. Every now and then we would go to a deserted spot outside the city, park and smoke bout a hundred joints then get back in the cars and ride up and down the strip again. Finally they'd drop me off. After two weeks of that Lou was like "Holmes", that's what they called me, "Holmes."

"Holmes my moms and pops wanna meet you. They want you to come over and have dinner wit us."

I was like "cool." I hadn't ate a home cooked meal in months, maybe years. I went over and I didn't really know what to expect but when I walked in I was surprised to see it looked just like our house except for the family pictures on the wall where different. Lou's pops was hella cool and his moms was a real sweet lady.

"My son tells us you're from California and you came way down here to work. You're a long way away from home son."

"Yes ma'am."

"So how do you like our town" she asked wit an accent I really had never heard before.

"It's alright, it's different but it's cool. I like it."

"So how long do you plan on stayin?"

"Well I'll be here until the job is over ma'am."

"Son, you came here to save money right?"

"Yes ma'am."

"Well how can you do that livin in that high priced motel?"

"I'll be alright."

"Louis tells us you're a good guy. You can come and stay wit us and save your money."

I sat there wit my mouth open. I couldn't believe it. These people were openin there house to me and didn't even know me!

"Thank you ma'am, but I can't impose on y'all like that."

"Well you can at least come over on Sundays and eat you a good meal."

"Now I promise you I will do that!"

She smiled and we all laughed. They could tell home cooked meals was far and few between for me.

"You like the Cowboys" his pops asked. I had forgot he was even there.

"N'all, I can't lie I can't stand them. My teams is the Raiders and the 49ers."

"Well you make sure you come over here Sunday so you can watch the Cowboys beat the mess outta the Raiders."

I promised him I would, and then ate some of the best food I ever ate in my life.

After that night I was at their house every Sunday, watchin football and eatin some of the best Mexican food I ever tasted.

I worked at that job for another six months before movin to Albuquerque, the biggest city in New Mexico. Lou drove me to the gas station where the Greyhound Buses stopped.

"Holmes when you comin back?" Lou said, sittin in his '69 Impala.

"I don't know but I promise I'll never forget you and your folks.

We family. Make sure you tell your mom and dad I said thanks for everything."

"Maybe when you get settled in I can come up there and kick it wit you." I could tell he didn't want me to leave. Really I didn't want to go either but I knew I had to go. It was no more work.

"Holmes you take it easy and call me when you get there" Lou said as I got outta the car.

"Fo sho Lou, peace." It felt like I was leavin my brotha. In that short time we had really bonded. I stayed in touch wit the Trujillo family for years until I started goin to prison and lost contact.

Ridin the bus to Albuquerque was kinda spooky. It was night and it was no lights on the highway. The background outside the window was pitch black and my ears were filled wit Spanish, spoke by the families on their way to the big city. Finally, in the distance I saw lights flickering and as the wheels turned the blurred lights became clearer. We were approachin Albuquerque. After pullin into the bus station I got my bags, got a room and the next mornin I was out lookin for me some work. I found this construction site.

"Excuse me sir are y'all doin any hiring?" I said to a skinny man wit glasses and a hard hat.

"What type of work are you lookin for?"

"Well, I finish concrete, lay bricks, do electrical and whatever you need done."

"Well, I tell you what. You be here in the mornin at 7 AM and I'll give you a shot. If you know what you doin you got 40 hours a week."

"Thank you very much, I'll see you in the mornin." Just that fast I was on my feet. It wasn't bout doin the work, I knew he would be impressed. All I needed was the opportunity.

CHAPTER 3

The whole time I kept writin my thoughts and my rhymes. After being in the city for bout four months, I met this dude at a park smokin weed. I was sittin on a bench and over walked this slim cat wit red hair, a Carolina blue Kangol on and a radio danglin from his hand.

"What's up partna what you on" he asked.

"I'm chillin man, what's happenin?"

"Ah shit, they call me Hollywood Supreme. I ain't never seen you around here before."

"Yeah I just moved up here from California."

"Fo real? I got family in LA."

"I'm from the Bay homey."

"Where that's at?"

"Oakland and San Francisco."

"So what brought you down here?"

"I needed some work. I just left a job in Clayton then I came here."

"Shit I need me a job my nigga. Can you help me get one?"

"They just hired me at this construction site up the street. I can show you where it's at."

"Damn you lucky nigga. Let me hit that weed."

I wasn't lucky, I knew I had a angel watchin over me. And I wasn't trippin on the nigga leechin off my weed, he was bout to be my guide into this ghetto. I passed it to him and this cat had vacuum lungs! I never seen nobody hit weed that hard in my life. After he blew the smoke out he turned his radio on, played an instrumental and started rhymin. I couldn't believe what I was hearing, this nigga right here was dope! When he finished I told him "I rhyme too homey."

"Is that right"

I went into my rhyme and he seemed to be feelin it. At the time I called myself MC FLOYD and before we left we decided to form a crew. We settled on the name The Fresh Force.

This was the early '80s, before crack hit the ghetto. We use to chill in the Kirk neighborhood near the Kirtland Air Force Base, in the northern section of Albuquerque, near where Supreme lived. It was 90% a black neighborhood, so I adapted quickly to the scene. Everyday we sat in his room listenin to LL Cool J, smokin weed and writin rhymes. At the time it was no west coast or down south influence in rap so our style was like RUN DMC and LL COOL J's. I was workin still and got Supreme workin at the construction company wit me. Eventually I saved up enough money to get a car and after that we were out on the town every weekend, hittin all the local parties, rhymin and shit. Supreme was a true b-boy nigga. The nigga could pop, DJ, freestyle and everything. See my whole plan was to go where ever I had to to get money enough money to move back to California on my own, record me a professional demo and eventually get into the music business. I didn't know a lot bout it at the time but I knew it took money to make moves in the game I wanted so badly to be in.

"Floyd you know homey you got a cool voice, but you gotta get your style down. One song you sound one way then on another song you sound another."

"What you mean" I asked, never havin noticed what he was talkin bout.

"When you rap, change your voice into a different tone than the one you're talkin in" and he went into a spiel.

"See what I mean?"

"Yeah, now I do."

"And then at certain points add your original voice to change up the flava."

At the time I was just learnin from him and we never went into a studio and actually recorded a record. After a while Supreme and I felt like we weren't gonna make it in this city. But Supreme wasn't gonna leave New Mexico.

One day at my job I met this brotha who was on another crew. The homey was hella swoll, look like he had just got out the pen.

"Whatup black" he said walkin towards the water cooler where I was standing.

"Man, just tryin to get it fam."

"My name's Arnold. Arnold Allen."

"They call me Floyd homey." I had started usin my middle name due to my MC status.

"How long you been workin here?"

"Shit, bout four or five months now homey."

"You from here?"

"N'all, I'm from Cali. The Bay homey"

"Damn. What u doin way down here?"

"Tryin to survive, cousin. Tryin to survive."

"Check this out, you smoke weed?"

"Hell yeah."

"After work let's kick it."

"That sound like a winner to me." The homey Arnold had a hot azz Trans Am. Blue wit rims and a T-top. Turned out he had a Mexican wife, his high school sweet heart, a little brotha named Ronnie and a fine azz sista named Regina. I usta kick it wit them real tough when I wasn't wit Supreme. This was pretty much my family. A few months passed and I heard bout a job in Rock Springs, Wyoming.

"Supreme, it's like this homey: the job here bout to end and they payin $18 an hour at this one in Wyoming. I gotta get it homey, you welcome to come."

"Nigga is you crazy? What the fuck I'mma do up there?"

"Shit. Stack paper so we can go to Cali and make a record."

"Man hell n'all. I'll be here when you get back" he had a look on his face like what I was talkin bout was the craziest shit in the world.

"I'mma holla at you when I get back then." We hugged and I knew that probably would be the last time I ever seen him.

I got the job and all I did was stack my chips so I could move back to the West. I'll always love the country but at that age, the fast track had me. I couldn't wait to get back to those Cali streets. We worked twelve hours a day six days a week and lived in the town of Rock Springs. The job was twenty miles outside the city so we got up at like 4 every mornin and rode a bus to work, then rode back, ate dinner, slept and then went back to work. It wasn't shit in the town but oil refinery workers, a gas station, police station and one restaurant. I couldn't wait to get back to civilization. Every now and then I would call Supreme to check on him. One day the supervisor told us that the job would be ending tomorrow and we would have a 40 hour check waitin on us at the gate.

I was happy as fuck, I was on my way back to Oakland California, up in the hills wit my grandparents! My Grandfather was a retired veteran of the Navy, so they were straight, but he was also military minded and that shit drove me nuts. My grandma, Big Mama, loved me unconditionally, I was her heart. She didn't always agree wit everything I did but she loved me regardless. So here I was sittin in the den on the couch across from my grand father, Big Mama was sleep in the other room. I had arrived early that evening.

"So Robert, what do you plan on doin wit yourself?" he said in his deep thunderous voice.

"Right now I just wanna chill for a few days, relax then I'mma go back to work."

"No son. I mean what are you gonna do wit your life?"

"Big daddy, I'm gonna be a rapper."

"A rapper," he said, wit a look of amazement on his face and laughin at the same time.

"Have you lost your damn mind boy?"

"No sir, that's what I wanna be."

"Well first of all that's takes money son."

"That's what I'm workin for: to save up money for studio time."

"So you mean to tell me you plan on stayin here for free and savin your money to go to the damn studio?"

"I thought y'all would be proud of me and would encourage me to pursue my dreams."

"What I and your grandmother want to see you do is go to college and make a life for yourself."

"Big Daddy, I want that too but I feel like what I been through in life was college."

"Son you really don't realize how hard we have worked so you can be sittin over there on that couch for free," he said in a disgusted voice.

I guess at the time I really didn't understand. I knew I wanted to be a rapper, that's all.

Plus I wasn't feelin all that being up in the hills shit. I wanted to be in the hood. If only I knew what was waitin down the hill for me. I had come up on an oil refinery job in Martinez, CA where I made good bread. One day my grandfather and I got into it and he decided it was time for me to go.

"Robert you need to pull your pants up walkin round here like that" he said as I walked past his room.

"Damn you be gettin on my nerves" I said under my breath, thinkin he didn't hear me.

"What did you say" I could hear him gettin out of bed. I knew it was bout to be some shit.

"Nothin, I didn't say nothin."

"Boy who do you think you raisin your voice at?"

"You the one hollering. I just got off work. I'm tired. I don't really feel like hearing this."

"This what, huh? This what?" Now he all up on me.

"This what? This bullshit man, this bullshit!" I just snapped. It came out before I knew it.

"I think it's time for you to find somewhere else to stay. Your britches gettin mighty big up in here boy."

"Whatever. I knew you wanted to kick me out anyway. You just been waitin to have a reason."

"I didn't have to let you live here from the jump. That's your damn problem. You think somebody owe you something."

"Yeah whatever. You won't have to worry bout me no more."

I knew my grandmother was gonna be mad at him for puttin me out and if I would've said I'm sorry I could have stayed but I was like "fuck this shit", grabbed my stuff and got the hell outta there. I was feelin like a man, so I went and got me a hotel room and called this breezy I knew.

"Hello" she answered on the first ring.

"Lil mama what's up?"

"Nothin."

"What u doin?"

"Layin down."

"Look, me and my granddaddy got into it and he told me to leave. I'm at this hotel on Macarthur. Get up, get dressed and come through."

"What's the name of the hotel and room number?"

"The Elks. Room 134" I was layin back on the bed, tryin to catch my breathe, exhausted from all the arguing me and big daddy had been doin.

For a minute it was the shit livin the hotel life, until I realize what it was costin me. That was around the same time crack hit. I had started smokin coke and weed – gremmies – and the next thing I knew, I lost my job and ended up in San Francisco.

CHAPTER 4

I stayed in this neighborhood called the Tenderloin, unlike any in the world. The streets were littered wit dope fiends and rundown hotels lookin like they were bout to collapse. The sound of sirens, arguments, catcalls, and children mixed into one, filling your eardrums. The police rounded the corners every 20 seconds. Urine, shit, crack smoke, Chinese food and a little corner store chicken was the constant aroma. The bus stop was a rest stop for heroine users, where they could get their nod on. The look of being lost was in most people eyes. Either that, or danger and relentlessness.

Some people called it the last drug haven in the U.S. You had muthafuckas smokin crack, shootin dope and women sellin pussy right out in the open. Wide open, like it wasn't nothin. It was youngstas down there gettin money, some from different parts of the city but it was also a core group of youngstas that lived in the community. This was their hood, their home and after being down there awhile these where the people who embraced me. Homeys like Jesse Clyde (now servin 25 to life), Gigolo Joe, Moose, Little Man Lattice, Trina, Tiny, Shante, Elray, Twoine, Money Ray, Ramone, (the twins) Terry and Larry a.k.a. Dug, my nigga Tony Coleman who always rep the T.L. the homey Chill, Psycho D (R.I.P), Little Jay, Duane, Cornell, Moe, My homey from Peru, Shadow who always had my back till this day and always got money (what up Blood) Samantha, Little Paul, T-Bone, Peanut, Kiesha, Misty, Tricie, T-Top, Filipino Charley, Jay {R.I.P} Cherry, Lady, Alice, Dodi, Mary, Rene, Chris, Charles, Nima, Nicole, Cyco Mike, Wendy, Price, Jerome, Roshaun, Eugene, Netta, Lisa, Alf, Woody, my Oakland kinfolk Sam, Roger the Dodger, Ricky Landerth and last but not least my nigga Bizzy muthafuckin Ben, one of the coldest hustla's in the west, to this day one of the best friends I got and will ever have. You can still find us, Dug, Tony together on the regular makin positive moves in the community.

Back then I kept me a sack full of that shit. It wasn't nothin to have a rack in my pocket daily and after a while, the breezy's noticed the potential. It was one who called herself Classy. She was a young hooker, half Black, Korean and Italian. One day I was on the block and she came up to me. I knew she was hoing and I wasn't wit that trick shit. She was like "what's your name?" in a kinda sexy way.

"If you gonna pay me for my time you takin up, you can call me whatever you want to call me." I said it so fast it threw her off guard. She started laughin to play it off so I turned around and started walkin away. She grabbed my arm.

"I wanna be wit you. I been watchin you, I like the way you carry yourself." And she came outta her bra wit a wad of bills. I had seen that move on the movie "The Mack". I didn't even count it. I stuffed it in my pocket and started to walk away.

She grabbed my arm again and was like "So what's your name?"
I said "you tell me."
"You ride like a Fleetwood so that's what I'mma call you. You hard but you smooth. I likes that."

Just that fast I was in the Mack Game. After her I had a female name Candy, a super bad Puerto Rican. One day she came and sat down beside me in a restaurant.

"You need you a real bitch and here I am."

"Is that right?"

"Yeah that's right now what you gonna do wit me?"

"First thang you need to do is act like you at the police station and empty out all your pockets and hand me all your possessions immediately" I said it without a smile and didn't blink, not once. She took all her jewelry off first then went into her panties and put a roll of money on the table, kissed me on the cheek, said "I'll be back daddy" and walked out the door, wit a lotta future behind her.

Now Candy was different. She was smart. from Hawaii, short thick as fuck wit a million dollar smile. She had come from LA and she usta always tell me that Dr. DRE and NWA was her homeys. Come to find out she wasn't lyin.

Candy was special to me I can't lie, she had me in love wit her. I broke the pimp code a few times when it came to her. The last time I seen her we was in a hotel room and she was three months pregnant. I left her to make a run, got jacked and ended up doin 6 months.

It wasn't my first time being locked down, that was when I was twelve in Martinez, California fuckin around wit my dad. I broke into his room to get some weed when he was outta town, then I had got caught up again in North Carolina but this was the first time I had ever been locked down and I was in love, a no no, so the shit was hard time, feel me? Two weeks before I was bout to get out she got busted and they extradited her back to Hawaii. She had ran away and when I finally spoke to her she was like "Daddy I don't wanna live like that anymore." I could hear the love in her voice and the want for change.

"Lil mama I understand. I'll always love you."

Those were the last words we shared before she hung up. I never saw the baby or heard from her again. Now while she was in lock up she told this half breed breezy to take care of me when I come home. I got out and I was comin up the block and saw this bowlegged red bone.

"Damn O.G. who is that" I asked to an old head I usta look out for.

"Oh that's this young renegade, been runnin round here for the last week or two shakin that thang" he said wit saliva drippin out his mouth. At that point she crossed the street and headed towards us. The closer she got the more money I could see in my future. When she got up to me I stepped to her.

"You know you gonna fuck around and get sued out here, movin them hips like that without some insurance on your azz." I didn't even think bout smilin.

"Is that right? And how you know that?"

"Because accidents happen all the time from people who don't know how to drive."

"What the hell you talkin bout?"

"If you out here doin all that you doin, and don't know what you doin, you gonna get done in. Feel me?"

"Nigga what's your name?"

"First let me ask you something. You afraid of heights?"

"Hell n'all."

"Well this your lucky day. You bout to come up then, fuckin wit me. They call me Fleetwood."

"You Fleetwood?"

"The one and only baby."

"I been lookin for you. Candy told me to take care of you, here you go daddy. I promise I'll do better. You watch and see."

As she walked off I played it off like I knew what was goin on but I had no idea why this bowlegged red bone had just gave me her money. But I was on the track and people had their straws all in the air. Eyes was on me so I had to play it like that. But after a while she got to fuckin up. Chippin wit that hop and just became a headache.

I wasn't really into that pimp shit. I was a dope boy. I wasn't really into waitin on no broads to bring me no money. Plus it was too many headaches. And I had little sisters. That shit just didn't sit right wit me. So finally I was like fuck that shit. I went back to sellin just crack. And spent the next four years of my life in and out of the San Francisco County Jail.

The 6th floor jail at 850 Bryant St. was damn near like being on the streets. You had your clothes on and if you was a hustla you had your hustle on. Everything that was on the streets was in there but your freedom. Upstairs the 7th floor was a little more serious. You had niggaz on their way to the pen and awaitin trial. Most niggaz went from the 7th floor to San Bruno – the county jail. This was something like a scene from the movie Gladiator. 6 tiers on both sides, a big azz yard and a gang of niggaz from all different sets and turfs in the city. If you had on yellow you were sentenced, white meant you worked in the kitchen and orange was still waitin to go to court. Niggaz was constantly gettin their azz whooped. Wasn't no pistols in there either. If you weren't wit your homeys you was fucked. I got into a few little scraps but but I held my own. After that niggaz pretty much left me alone. I stayed to myself and every time I would go to Bruno I would start to write again. I think it was my second visit, doin one year for drug possession, when I met this dude named "Honest Bob."

One day I was on the tier writin and this dude from Fillmoe was like "homey what you doin?" wit a smirk on his face.

"Just puttin a few rhymes together."

"Let me hear something." So I spit bout 8 lines and I could tell he was plottin on something.

"Look, I got my homey Honest Bob and he'll smash you partna."

"Is that right? Go get 'um"

Five minutes later, in walks this short dude, pimpin hella hard like he was bout to slaughter me. At that time of the day you could go from tier to tier, so Bob walks up.

"You Fleetwood?"

"Fo sho'."

"Let me hear you rhyme" he said, tryin to test my waters.

"You go ahead and spit something."

"They told me you wanted to battle me."

I wasn't wit all that back and forth gibberish. I was like I'mma smash this little arrogant nigga, make him and his homey tuck their tale. I wasn't really wit that battlin shit on the street and I knew in jail niggaz get into feelings quick, so a battle was a quick way to get some shit started but fuck it. I started bustin hard for bout two minutes. At the time LL was the shit and that's who I had came up on. LL and Too $hort. I heard him on the side line talkin to his homey.

"He rap like LL Cool J. Man I got him" I heard him say.

Finally I finished. Bob just looked at me and started rhymin. Right in the middle of his verse he started singin, then went right back to rhymin. He must have did that shit fo bout ten minutes. He killed it I admit and at that moment I knew I had to step my game up. He had smashed on me and I was a fighter and I didn't believe in losin. It cut me in a way and he embarrazzed me even though niggaz told me I held my own. Fuck that I didn't like that shit but I knew he could teach me shit so I played it smooth. This was part of my hip hop growth.

After he finished I was like "Where you from homey?"

"I'm from all over the bay I grew up in Oakland and Fillmoe" he said.

"Yeah, where?"

"My family live in the Bankers."

"I'm from Page St. Man you dope my nigga, I ain't even gone lie."

"Thanks homey. You got skills too, you just gotta develop styles."

"What you mean?"

For the next couple months Bob and me would sit and vibe. They had moved him to our tier so it was convenient. That nigga was our radio. At night he was the first person I ever heard sing gangsta hooks. This was before Nate Dogg, plus Honest could rhyme like a muthafucka. He taught me how to actually construct a rap song. This was the birth of my style.

One day I was on the yard and these cats from Lakeview, a hood in the Sco, walked up to me and was like "you Fleetwood?"

"Yeah, what's up?"

These wanna be Run-DMC niggaz went off in a routine bout my fake Stacy Adams and how I was a wanna be pimp. See, I had got caught up wit a pink pinstripe suit on and had come to jail wit it, includin my Stacy Adams. I didn't even know these niggaz, had never even seen them before. I guess my name was floatin around the jail as a rapper or whatever. But right in the middle of their routine this light skin nigga wit freckles walked up and started bustin hard as fuck and shut them niggaz up quick. This cat name was Frisco Kid and he had a record out called "Servin 'Um." He gave me a studio hook up for when I got out but I was still stuck in that drug life.

The street has many addictions. As soon as I got out I was like "fuck probation" and I walked right back up the street to downtown San Francisco like I had never left. I had my same pink suit on and the Stacy's. The suit was hella tight because I had gained weight, you know how jail do you. I needed some gear and I knew how I was gonna get it. I had to go find my niggaz quick. I didn't understand it at the time but I was strung out on power. The power that the block gave me wit a few hoes and a sack full of crack. The money was only a part of the play. Take into consideration this was when crack was big so in a weird way it seemed like the thing to do. Later in my life I would learn that I was a pawn in the government's drug game.

I was out hustlin for a high for no more than 3 months, dodgin the police, keepin ounce money, never really comin all the way up. Before I knew it I was right back in San Bruno for violation of probation. This time it felt different. By this time in my life I had been in Bruno so many times I damn near knew every guard by name and they knew me. I was tired of that shit, the food, the jail house lies, the commissary, the constant frustration that you stay in the midst of that causes fights everyday. The fact that you have no form of privacy. I was just tired of all that shit. I guess I knew my next stop was the big house. When I finally went to court I had already been down six months. They gave me another year but didn't allow me jail credit for time spent prior to trial. It was takin that or 3 years in the penitentiary. So I actually did 14 months in the county. Eight for the year and six I had already done.

My out date came around and it was time to hit the streets again. The most anticipated moment is when you bout to get out and the punk azz guard takin his time because he knows you in a hurry to leave. When they hand you your clothes they're always too tight because you done gained weight while being down. You squeeze into those tight azz clothes and wait for them to call your name to go out the door.

While I was dressin, two feds came in, sayin they had a warrant for my arrest for another probation violation.

CHAPTER 5

Between the time I lost the oil refinery job and when Big Daddy had put me out I usta work at the PX across the bridge in Alameda where the souljas shopped. Big Mama had got me the job there cleanin up. I usta come in hella early and put a gang of Adidas sweat suits in a garbage can, roll them out and hide them by the dumpster in a empty box, come get them later and go to San Francisco and get my hustle on. One mornin I came to do my thang and as soon as I pushed the garbage can through the door the buzzers went off. They had got hip to me and had put buzzers under all the garbage cans. It was a wrap and I was hella embarrazzed. Big Mama had to come get me from the brig and she was hot as fish grease! When I went to court they gave me one year probation, but I was like "fuck that." I went back across the bridge to San Francisco and started hustlin. Big Mama didn't say nothin, she just dropped me off at the BART station and told me to be careful.

Now they had finally caught up to me and it was like time had stopped. Their voices sounded like they were talkin in slow motion. I kept waitin to wake up, but this was real as fuck. I sat in the back of a fed car headed for federal holdin at 850 Bryant. I was mad, like I had lost the winnin lottery ticket. Instead, they gave me my orange jump suit.

I walked in the quad and looked between those oh so familiar bars, saw the steel toilet, the steel benches and the steel bunks. My nostrils filled wit the smell of feet and underarms mixing wit bad breath, piss and shit. It was no mystery, I was headed back to the 7th floor. I was housed in the federal holdin tank, but really it was the same shit. The news was on talkin bout this big drug bust in Oakland. They had snatched some cat by the name of Little D. I had heard of him in Oakland. Niggaz use to scream "Fuck the World, Love Little Darryl!!" He was from the notorious 69 Village, nephew of the drug czar Felix Mitchell. Definitely a hitter. Even though I grew up in Oakland at the time I stayed in downtown Frisco in the T.L. so I had never really seen him or nothin like that. Anyway, I see this dude watchin the news.

"What's up homey where you from?"

"I'm from from Oakland" he said in a low voice.

"Yeah, I guess you see they just got one of the ballas, Lil D, over there in Oakland wit 26 pounds of yay."

"Nigga that's me" he said.

"Look you ain't got to lie to kick it" I said laughin.

Right then the news broadcast showed his picture on the screen. "Nigga that's me, my name is Darryl Reed" he said, wit authority this time.

We was locked down in that Fed quad for 3 months and we got to be homeys. This was one of the most intense, laid back cats I had ever met in my life. He didn't eat any meat, he loved to watch the horse races and read the paper. We use to talk a lot, play dominoes and just do whatever we could to pass the time. The feds was sending under covers in, tryin to frame him. We use to laugh at the little games they played. My court date came and they ordered me to a federal halfway house until my next court date.

I told D "Fam I'm up. I'm bout to go to this house in east Oakland. Hold your head up. I'll stay in touch. Real talk."

"Fleet whatever you do, when you get out, stay out. This ain't for you homey."

It was like he was lookin through me but lookin at me at the same time. We exchanged pounds and the bars slid open.

The halfway house was located in east Oakland and I stayed there for three days. I received a pass to go and see my P.O. (Probation Officer) in downtown Oakland and I jumped on the train wit the old thoughts – "fuck the police" – even though originally I had decided to try something different. Being down an extra 90 something days had brought back the "fuck that" attitude. I sat on the train wit Oakland passing by, the train headed into the tunnel, under the water into San Francisco. All I could think of was "here we go again." It was their job to catch me and my job not to let them. At that time I was still rhymin but I was lost in the drug game, on my way to becomin institutionalized tryin hard to tread water, feel me? It was like the game was keepin me out of focus. It tends to do that even though you know you need focus to come up.

I had no respect for law or any form of authority. I just didn't give a fuck. It was something bout authority that I didn't like. I guess I had just been on my own too long wit no discipline and didn't like anyone tellin me what to do. It always seemed that the ones tellin me what to do was white people or some Uncle Tom niggaz and wit my knowledge of slavery, I definitely felt they gave less of a fuck bout me. I realized later in life that it's more than one way to skin a cat and I was fightin against myself. Goin at the system like that I was never gonna win. See, as long as you in the system you can't beat the system. It's all bout deception wit them, you never let them know how you feel till it's too late.

So there I was again, back in the mix but after bout two weeks it got old. The NARC'S had my picture. I could only come out at night and one night they crept up and it was all over. I was on my way back inside. As soon as I got back in the orange suit, I was walkin through the cell block. The first person I seen was Little D. He was still waitin on trial. He looked at me through the bars and shook his head wit a look of surprise mixed wit disgust.

"Fleet, what the fuck you doin back up in here?"

"I tricked that halfway house off fam."

"Yeah I see. So did they catch you dirty?"

"N'all just that abandon charge and the failure to appear."

"Nigga you lucky as fuck. When you gonna start valuin your freedom? The next time you might not get that damn lucky." There was that look again. Through me but at me.

"Okay now that's enough of that jaw jackin. Keep it movin" said the guard noticin me standing by the bars.

"Yo D I'mma shoot you a kite alright?"

"Fo sho'" was the last words I heard from him. 15 years later Master P and me would chop it up bout Little D in North Carolina during an interview.

Here I was again in federal holdin waitin on trial. I spent most of my days writin and just thinkin bout the stupid situation I had got myself into. I really didn't know what to expect goin to court. In jail that's what stresses you out the most, besides being in love. When you're awaitin trial, you don't know what's bout to happen.

My day came and I gave the judge a sad story. She fell for it and sentenced me to 90 days in the federal prison. I can't lie I was nervous as fuck on that Grey Goose, that's what they called the bus. I had been to many institutions but never a federal prison, even though it was said to be a lot easier time, just knowin I was goin around lifers made me uneasy, feel me? When I got on the bus the inside was like the inside of that prison plane "Con Air." Cages and more cages lined up on the walls. Contraptions to bolt us down to the chairs individually and a bullet proof glass cubicle surroundin the drivers seat.

They had chains around my ankles and waist plus I was handcuffed and didn't know where the hell I was goin. After a long bus ride from San Francisco in the wee hours of the night we finally reached the destination. As we pulled into an underground garage it looked like we were downtown somewhere but I didn't know. I hadn't held any conversations the whole way down from S.F. I was a long way from home and wasn't around any of my homeys. When the bus stopped we were shuffled off into a building. It looked like a tall office building but like the five top floors had gated plateau's, not knowin that that would be where I spent most of my time. I heard someone say we was in downtown L.A. I found out later that I was in a new federal prison called MDC.

They took us through the usual procedure, looking up a niggaz azz, all that shit. They gave me an ID number and some brown khaki's. As I stood and looked around, it didn't feel like a jail. No bars anywhere to be seen; it was more similar to a college dorm wit a basketball court adjacent to it. I got settled in and started minlin around tryin to get a better feel for the place. I walked through the sally port, tryin not to have eye contact or come off like I was the toughest nigga in there nor come off like I was soft either. I was just kinda gettin a feel for the place. That's when I saw this dark skin nigga wit a gold chain on. The chain was thick as hell wit a cross on it. I was like "what kinda jail is this these niggaz got jewelry on" and I also noticed it looked kinda like he had on gold rimmed glasses. Real gold. I couldn't believe the shit. Damn, how this nigga get that shit in here? The hours in the day was passing. I ate whatever they fed me and we started hoopin. There was this chubby dude shootin by himself. I walked up and introduced myself to him. "What up homey, my name Fleetwood."

"They call me Bo. Fleet what you know bout this ball right here?"

"I'm from Cali homey but I also grew up in Carolina. Shitted, that's all we do is ball." I took a few steps towards him and attempted to steal the ball. I could tell that he had some skills by his maneuvering.

"Yo, lets shoot some twenty one" I said.

"Now you sure you wanna do that to yourself lil homey" Bo asked, smilin like he knew he was gonna win.

"Don't worry I won't break but one of your ankles Bo" I said smilin the whole time.

"Oh it's on, now go ahead and start it off " I walked to the free throw line as he passed me the ball and began the game. I hit my first six shots, that's when Bo kicked it in gear. This big ol chubby negro was fast like Barkley when he was in college. Big but agile.

After he tied the score he went ahead three points. That's when I had had enough. I stole the ball and shook him twice, went straight to the hoop. I couldn't dunk but it was still pretty. I crossed him up and had him stumblin backwards tryin to regain his balance as I blew passed him. For the next few minutes we went back and forth. I had just scored and was walkin towards the foul line. I looked over and noticed that there was a small crowd watchin us the whole time.

Then out the corner of my eye, I saw that dark skin nigga wit the gold chain come out. I noticed when he came in, the crowd parted to let him through like he wasn't to be fucked wit. That's when it clicked that this nigga had some power in this joint and definitely on the streets. As Bo and I continued our game, the dark skinned cat started fuckin wit Bo because of the fact that I shook him a couple of times.

"Little black takin you Bo?" he said. Then I looked up and locked eyes wit this dark skin dude .

"Black I got my chips on you" he said and I nodded. I ended up beatin Bo and afterwards the dark skinned dude came up to me.

"You can ball little homey, what's up, where you from?"

"Thanks playa, they call me Fleetwood, I'm from the Bay Area."

"They wrapped you huh?"

"Yeah on some bullshit. I just left Little D up in Frisco jail."

"Well they call me Mike if you need something holla at me. I gotcha."

"I'm cool but thanks though" I knew better than to accept anything from anybody in the pen.

"It ain't no strings attached lil homey. I recognize a soulja when I see one" he smiled and walked off.

After that whole introduction, they kinda took me under their wing. We use to chop it up, eat and play ball together. After my third day in prison, we were all sittin in the T.V room. Bo was on one side of me and Mike was on the other. The LA news had a story on the most notorious drug lords in the country and how they had been apprehended for drug possession and murder. Four pictures popped up and the anchor men announced the names: Bo Bennett, Michael

"Harry O" Harris, Freeway Ricky Ross and a Columbia dude, Mario Biluano. They were showin all the dope, guns and money they had, that was seized along wit all their territories.

I couldn't believe it, here I was sittin right between both of these niggaz. They were like Kingpins for real. At first I didn't even look at either of them. I froze up like an ice cube. I looked over a Bo and saw that he had a blank stare fixed on the T.V screen. Harry O looked at me and then smiled. He smiled as if he wasn't sweatin that shit to the least. At the time, Harry O was worth 30 million dollars. He had funded the first black play on Broadway in 1987–88. I couldn't believe that I had two Scarface type niggaz treatin me like I was their little brother. I knew I was straight but I knew I had to play it smooth. The following mornin I was talkin to Harry O bout life and I mention to him "Mike I wanna be a rapper. I know I can make it."

"Fleetwood that's a hard business" he said wit no sugar coatin on it. "You bout to be dealin wit some corporate gangsta shit and their whole science is to find someone wit talent who can't afford to make a record, because it do cost."

"What you mean?"

"To promote a record costs. Videos, ad's and payin radio to play your shit. All that."

"Okay I see what you sayin."

"And what they do is have you sign your talent away to them for a little of nothin. Basically, it's all based on exploitation: findin someone blinded by the glitz and fame of the game and then fuckin them outta everything while they live the life of a star: the jewelry and cars which most of the time belong to the record company."

He put his palms out up as if to emphasize it like "that's the truth."

"So my advice to you would be to study the game. Learn how to own your own masters you understand?"

"Most definitely."

Harry O on the real gave me my first lesson bout the music biz, the inside of it at a point where I could really understand what he was sayin. It made me understand that I had to be on my P's and Q's if I was gonna fuck wit this shit or I was gonna end up rappin for free. But it only made me wanna rap even more now because I knew what it would take to make it. Now all I wanted to do was read as much as I could bout the game. Just the thangs Harry O told me always kept my straws up and my curiosity hungry, feel me? He didn't have to school me and that's why I'll always have love for him, believe that shit nigga.

So after that I spit some of my rhymes to him. He encouraged me to stay at it and keep tryin. "Look, when you get out homey I got a plug for you. Just be patient and I'mma holla at ya. As the days rolled by, Harry O and I continued to kick it. I never pressured him bout the plug he had for me. I figured we would be there for awhile.

One late night the guards woke me up without warning. They told me to get my belongings because I was being transferred. An hour later, I was on a Grey Goose headed to somewhere; I didn't have a clue. I was hella mad because I didn't get to holla at Bo and Harry O before I left. Harry O was the coolest gangsta muthafucka I had ever met. Quiet as hell, but you could tell he wasn't for any shit. You could also tell that he was very powerful at what he did. Bo was more outgoing, always smiling as if nothin bothered him.

I tried to contact Harry O, but never could reach him. The letters always came back. I found out that two weeks after I left Harry and Bo, Suge Knight started to visit and eventually, Harry O' gave Suge 1.5 million dollars to start Death Row Records. (In 2005, Harry won 106 million dollar lawsuit against Knight.)

Bolted from head to toe wit chains all around my body, tryin to hold my piss. I sat in this plastic chair on a Grey Goose headed to who knows where. I didn't think bout where I was goin and what was ahead of me. My only thoughts were "I'll never meet gangstas like them again."

CHAPTER 6

The sound of the bus brakes squealin and this big azz wall openin brought me out of my daze. I looked out the window and seen this building that looked like a Roman Castle. It was surrounded by layers of barbwire fences and guarded by white boy guards who coulda been linebackers, itchin to shoot a nigga. As they shuffled us off the bus, I began to realize that I was at the big house. This place was no joke. I saw this sign that said, "Maximum Security." Besides Death Row this was the cruelest form of incarceration. I couldn't believe this shit. I asked myself why the fuck they got me in here. I only was given 90 days. Maybe this was some kind of mistake or hopefully this was just orientation and I would be transferred within a few days.

We got the phone call and they escorted us all to this room, lined us up while this linebacker white boy walked in the room to scream at us as if we were children. "Welcome to Lompoc Federal Prison." He said. He laid down all the do's and don'ts. What would happen and what would not. Then he advised us to enjoy our stay at "this wonderful hotel provided by the government."

He also added that he liked us and wanted us transferred to the minimum security camp outside of the wall in a few days. Until then we would be in orientation, housed in the hole for our own protection from population. That meant being in the cell 23 hours a day wit only

30 minutes of recreation time and 30 minutes to shower. There was steam comin from the pipes atop the bars and each tier had mesh wire on top, supposedly, to prevent you from gettin thrown over. As I walked down the tier, inmates were at the bars eager to see the new fish. Others were kicked back on there bunks either watchin TV or in their own world tryin hard to escape their reality.

As they closed the cell door behind me, that feelin of being less human and more like an animal began to sink in. The first night I heard someone gettin beaten and raped. I couldn't even sleep, this mass murder nigga in the next cell to me. It felt like I was in a dungeon at the bottom of the prison. It had a foul smell to it, the water was brown and the toilets barely worked. Those few days we were suppose to be in there turned into two and a half weeks on the real. That shit felt like time had stopped. The mornin they told me to go get my shit, because I was goin to the farm, I couldn't believe it. Walkin through the corridors of that prison hole reminded me of one of those prison hardcore movies. It was niggaz yellin and hollering shit at us that were goin to the farm. Finally we made it to the big door that they had brought us through two weeks prior. As it opened the sun crept in. I finally saw the outside. Nature never looked more beautiful.

As they walked us across the street, I couldn't believe what I was seein: there were no fences, barbwire or anything. Prisoners were walkin around free and all. They took me to my dorm full of bunk beds and lockers. We went to the orientation for bout an hour then they took us to the chow hall. It was like a buffet, eat what you want as much as you liked in the allowed time given. I met some brothas and they wanted to introduce me to the others in the camp. They offered me hygiene products and asked me how long I'm stayin. I told them 15 and I guess they figured 15 years but I only had 15 days remainin on that sentence. For the next two weeks I did their prison work, played ball and tried to put my plan together for the streets. My out date came and it was time to go home. As I got my stuff together, a few of the homeys were shocked that I was leavin so soon.

"Homey where you goin" asked the brotha I had met first.

"Man that's it fo me family. Time for me to hit the streets" I said.

"What you got a early release or something?"

"N'all I was short when I came."

"For real?" he said, lookin at me like "why that couldn't be me."

"Look homey I appreciate the love y'all showed me. If it's anything I can do, this my address. Get at me." I was writin down my address as I was talkin.

"Just stay free black man, stay free."

"Fo sho', believe that."

He gave me a pound and started walkin away, the guards took me outside the fence and drove me to the bus station in Lompoc. It was a small town who's main income was the prison. That's all that was there, everybody and their mama worked at the prison. I didn't really meet anybody who was locked down from Lompoc at Lompoc but all the guards there were from the town so that told me enough. I definitely could tell I was far from the hood. The few people I saw wasn't scared, they knew I was fresh out by the clothes I had on. They seemed to be pissed off that I was leavin, it meant less work for them or someone they knew. One guy came outta the bus station and said "you just git out huh?"

"Outta where?" I said.

"Outta Lompoc, the big house."

"Yeah. What's up?"

"How and the hell did you get parole?"

"I didn't, I maxed out my time. You sure seem surprised."

"Yeah" he said "cause most people don't make parole."

As I stood their waitin on the bus, I weighed my options. I knew I wasn't gonna last sellin dope in the streets of San Francisco any longer. The NARC.'s knew me too well. I was burnt up and to be honest I was tired of the same old shit. It was 1989, and I wanted to get out of California.

Here I was, fresh out the feds, back on the block standing at the phone booth. I called Terry Lee Bracken, my cousin down south.

"Hello."

"What up cousin, this Weezy."

"Nigga I know who it is, pretty azz nigga." Since we was little, my cousin was the general: younger than me but always focused and had incredible self discipline and was far from being a punk. My uncle Booster was a legend in the town and the apple never falls far from the tree.

"Man it's ugly out here. I need to come back to the country."

"When you tryin to leave?"

"Shitted, within the hour."

"Call me back in two hours nigga"

The phone went dead and I stared at it. I knew I could always count on my cousin. And I always knew I could count on him to talk shit, that's how that nigga was. So that night I was on a Greyhound, headed for North Carolina.

It felt good to be on a bus without chains around my ankles and waist and in handcuffs, every now and then my eye would catch a speck of light through the window but mainly it was pitch black outside and my thoughts where consumed wit my future, it was finally back in my hands. Those three days on the bus gave me plenty of time to think bout what I was really gonna do. My thoughts were on rappin, and that was it. When the bus pulled in the station in Greensboro N.C., there stood my cousin Terry. My cousin and I had been tight since the 5th grade.

"Damn nigga you done got fat as hell!" he said.

"Man, fuck you nigga."

"I thought you said you was swoll?" This nigga never stopped talkin shit.

"Nigga I ain't fat look at your fat azz stomach."

"Boy this come from livin good."

"Well that's what I'm tryin to do, live good cousin. I ain't tryin to see no more cells."

"I hear ya boy. Ain't nobody fuck wit you in there did they?"

"Hell n'all. I mean I had a few scraps but that's how that goes. For the most part I was cool."

"So what you gonna do Rob?" He was one of the few people that still called me Rob. He usta call me "Black Rob" and there were people around the country that thought it was me singin that song "Whoa."

"Man I need to get me a job."

"What kinda work you lookin for?"

"Shit anything but I'mma need a car to get around."

"I gotcha my nigga don't trip."

"Cousin, you know what I really wanna do? I wanna rap."

"Can you rap?"

"Hell yeah nigga?"

I went straight into my rhyme book, he couldn't believe it.

"You need to go to New York but you gotta get your money up first."

"I feel ya."

"I got ya my nigga, I told'cha that."

The next day Terry brought me a car and I got a job at a factory. My whole life I never wanted to work in one of those buildings. Growin up I had seen my partna's mothers and fathers work at these places for years only to get laid off or fired, wit no other job experience. There wasn't a lotta room for advancement at these mills. Most promotions was based on who your family was and how long they had been workin there. When I walked in the inside reminded me of a prison work complex: a bunch of robots wit someone up top over lookin everyone. I usta wake up in the mornin dreadin going that place – the smell of it irked me – and the slave mentality, I just hated that shit. They had me loadin rolls of heavy shit into trucks when it came off presses. One day the mark azz supervisor told me I wasn't movin fast enough and my back was already hurtin. My nigga, I knew I wasn't gonna last at that shit.

I had been workin there for bout three weeks, and one day I went to lunch and was sittin in my car. I looked around and said to myself "this here is too far from the rap game for me." I rolled me a joint, turned Too $hort up, lit my weed, rolled the window down and yelled "bitchhhhhhhhhhhhhhhhh!!!" I threw the hard hat and safety glasses out the window and smashed off like "fuck you and this job." That night I sold my car and called my cousin and told him I was goin to

New York to pursue my dream. He was mad at the way I left but he understood.

I slept on the bus going to New York and when I woke up I was in Manhattan. Our first stop was Port Authority, Downtown New York. I walked out the bus station. This was the famous 42nd street (before they tore it down). The scene reminded me of downtown San Francisco: Hoes, dope, dealers and cracked out hotels everywhere. I went and got me a hotel room and I ended up stayin there for a week. I heard bout this rap contest that charged a $100 entrance fee wit the winner receiving a demo deal.

So I went to the spot and did my thing but the judges where rigged. The contest was won before I got there. I met this cat who had helped put it together; he was from Minnesota.

"Say brotha what's your name?" he said. I had seen him speakin to the judges all night.

"They call me Fleetwood."

"You know, a lotta these contests are popularity events instead of being based on talent."

"Yeah I realized I was fightin a losin battle when I noticed the scores some of them cats was gettin."

"You want a beer or something?"

"N'all I'm cool man I'mma holla." I still was in a strange city and I was startin to get the impression that this cat might be gay or something.

"Hold up Fleet, let me put a bug in your ear." He reached out, grabbin my arm.

"What's happenin wit'cha homey?" I said, pullin my arm away.

"Look, I think you got talent. Your style is fresh."

"Thanks man."

"Where you from?"

"I'm from California but I've lived in a few places."

"Look Fleet this would be my suggestion to you: go and nurture your style, study the game you in. Get your wordplay and rhyme scheme tight, then come back to NY because this place is a monster."

"What you mean?"

"Well if you came here to be a rapper, wit no job or connections in this game, you ain't gonna survive. It's gonna eat you alive."

I could hear the sincerity in this cat's voice. I started to really pay attention to what he was sayin.

"Fleet, I came here like ten years ago. I play the piano and drums. I had a audition at the Apollo. I had won in Minneapolis, that's where I'm from, and if I hadn't got involved in the promotions aspect of the game after my performance, I would probably be a dope fiend, in jail or dead like so many wanna be stars in the game."

"What made you decide to get into promotions" I asked him.

"After findin myself homeless so many times tryin to pay for studio time and rent together which don't work I decided to pursue a job in the music business that would keep me close to what I love. So now I promote these contests, some legit, some bogus. Straight up."

"At least you honest bout this shit."

"What I suggest is you go to Minnesota and stack your paper while you workin on your career. I don't know if you know it or not, but Minnesota has it own music scene wit the Time, Prince, Jimmy Jam, Terry Lewis and quite a few more people circulatin in that area."

"Yeah I heard of Prince, but I never looked at it like that."

"Fleetwood listen to me. I'm tellin ya, it would be the best move to make right now."

So there was a music hook up already in progress down in Minnesota. The downfall of Minnesota was that it was too cold during the winter, which lasts bout 8 months out of the year. I sat in that motel room lookin out the window at the rows and rows of skyscrapers. Even at night, the congestion of people in the city was obvious. People on top of each other, no room to breathe in this enormous concrete jungle. I stared at it for bout an hour. Then I finally decided to travel to Minnesota. within two hours, I was back in Port Authority, wit the workin class, homeless and hustlas passing through every minute of the day, on their way to somewhere. I had never felt so uncomfortable in a city in my life and I knew right then that I didn't wanna be there as I sat waitin on a bus to Minneapolis.

CHAPTER 7

When I got off the Greyhound in downtown Minneapolis, the first thing I noticed was how clean the streets were. Bout a second later I realized how cold it was – like 30 degrees. As I walked through downtown, I kept seein niggaz wit white girls. It wasn't something I had never seen before, but it was like 75% of the couples I was seein were mixed. The more and more I walked I noticed that all the buildings were connected to each other wit what I later learned was called a skyway due to how cold it gets. They try to keep people inside as much as possible. Finally I got tired of walkin around, I went and got me a room, settled in and started devising my come up.

I had learned the welfare game in San Francisco: how to get on G.A and use the city resources for a boost to get on my feet. I knew the first thing to do was to get into a shelter so you would seem like you definitely needed some help. Start at the bottom, so that's what I did. The following mornin I was in the welfare office and I couldn't believe what they was tellin me. Not only was they gonna to give me a check and food stamps, but also if I found an apartment that I could afford, they would pay the first and last months rent. Immediately after leavin there I registered at a temporary labor joint and went out and found me an apartment. Two days later I was livin in a cool one bedroom apartment on the Southside of Minneapolis on Pillsbury and 27th. It had nice lookin houses, kinda reminded me of the south, but wit alleys. And the grass in some yards was a big improvement over New York. I didn't know it at the time but I was in the heart of the crack hood, and dead smack in the center of gang territory. I would learn later down the road I was entering into a totally different culture.

A few days passed by and I saw a few niggaz and ho's floatin around but it still hadn't hit me yet. Then one night I was comin from the store and this broad ask me was I straight. I kept walkin bout another half a block and here comes some nigga and I could tell he was tweakin and he was like "You straight? You straight?" That's when it hit me.

"Nigga I'm in the hood. It's money out here."

That night I gave this old nigga twenty dollars to school me on what was really poppin in the streets. I quickly learned that the prices was tripled in Minnesota and the police were still tryin to find ways to stop niggaz gettin money. Now, wit my Tenderloin trainin I knew how I could come up quick but I had to get me a connect, or get on the Greyhound go to Cali and come back. My paper wasn't strong enough for that so I was gonna have to find someone in Minnesota until I could stack my paper so eventually I could go to Cali.

That next day I came outside my apartment building wit like $175. I saw a bunch of youngstas. One stood out and I could tell he was on his paper. I slid up on him to holler bout some work. The little homey's name was Brickhead (now servin a 26 year sentence). He was leery at first but then after talkin a few minutes he realized he was fuckin wit a real nigga.

A few days went by and I'm gettin my grind on stackin paper. I had heard bout this school, Brown Institute, that it was a good place to go for electronic engineering – how to dissect computers inside out. I figured I would learn this and it would pay for my studio time once I got a job at it, so I applied and got accepted in the electronic engineering coarse.

One night comin from school I entered my building and saw this cat that I had been servin. He was like "don't you fuck wit rap music" cause I usta be on the block free stylin. I was like yeah and he said his nephew just got up there from Gary, Indiana and he rap and he was cold. So I went down to his apartment and saw this little young nigga sittin on the couch. He was a light skinned young dude, dead on Warren G, and had a look in his eyes that said he had been through some shit.

"This Jason, my nephew."

We exchanged pounds and I was like "let me hear you spit."

After the fourth line I was hooked. This little nigga was dope for real. So after that me and Jason went back to my apartment, listened to some beats, rhymed, smoked some weed and just kinda bonded.

"They call me LP" he said.

"What that stand for?"

"Little Professor. They say I'm always in a book readin. Me and my moms moved up here for a better life."

"Where y'all from?"

"G.I. Gary, Indiana."

"Where Michael Jackson from?" I asked.

"Yeah but shit, I ain't never seen that nigga."

"Do he help the city out?"

"Fuck n'all. Gary fucked up 'wood. No jobs. All the steel mills closed and after that crack came. It's been ugly ever since. That was the main source of income. Now it's welfare and crack. Gary is a little Chicago. Plus it's infested wit gangs."

"Y'all got Crips and Bloods down there?"

"N'all, GD's and Vicelords"

"What's that?"

"GD's is 'Gangsta Disciples.' We ride under the six chief Larry Hoover, Vicelords ride under the five Willie Lord Peoples."

I didn't know what the fuck he was talkin bout. Everybody think Cali is full of gang bangers, but in Northern Cali we don't bang. It's bout hustlin and reppin your block, not no color.

"So y'all be trippin on colors?"

"Well GD's wear blue and black mostly and hats to the right. Vice-lords wear red and black and hats to the left. They mostly come from the Westside of Chicago and Disciples come from the Southside of' 'Go." I figured he was talkin bout Chicago. He told me he had shot heroin at age nine and I couldn't believe that shit. He was like it was just something to do. He told me that's how fucked up Gary was and I told him all bout Oakland and San Francisco's pimpin and hustlin scene and we just chopped it all night. Then I was like "Yo, let's start a group."

"Shit," LP said, "I'm wit that homey."

His moms had a apartment across the street and she was doin her thang. So when Jason wasn't in school, Jason and I was on the block gettin money or up in my apartment writin rhymes, smokin weed and fuckin broads. Eventually niggaz started callin us the Pillsbury Dope Boyz caused I had brought the tripled up dope concept from Cali and we was killin 'um. I had a solid plug and everything was straight. We shortened our street name to "The Dope Boys" and decided that should be the name of our group.

One night we was in my apartment chillin, doin what we do, and Jason kept turnin the music up hella loud.

"Yo Jason turn that music down some" I told him. I guess my instinct kicked in cause the next thing I heard was the sound of cattle. I knew that was mutha fuckas runnin toward me. The police. The NARCs. Me being in raids in Cali I knew what it was. I stuffed the sack.

"Jason hit the floor here they come" I told him wit a serious look on my face.

"Who" he said like "What you talkin bout?"

"The task force my nigga, get on the floor!"

"Wood, fo real?"

"Fo real my nigga. Don't say shit. Tell your name that's it."

The next thing I knew the door fell off and we got a formal in-troduction to the Minneapolis, MN. Task Force. A bunch of big azz white boys yellin wit guns pointin at my head "Don't move!!! Where the dope at!!!!"

According to them someone had just brought some drugs from my apartment. They tore the whole house up. Had us lyin on the floor in handcuffs and shit. I'll always remember the one cop sayin "We just killed one nigga you wanna be next?" Tycell Nelson was a young black man who had got murdered by the police like two days before.

"Look officer I don't sell no dope I go to school. There my books over there."

"Well somebody been sellin dope outta this apartment."

"Wasn't me" wit an "I ain't bullshittin" look on my face.

"Don't give me that shit!"

"Believe what you want to officer that's the truth."

"Well let me give you some truth. If dope keep comin outta this apartment, we will be back." As they got up from the kitchen table one of them punks had his foot on my couch wit his punk azz. They never failed to be azzholes, they never failed. My front door was fucked all up, hangin off the hinges, shit throwed everywhere, all my food in the cabinet on the floor. I think they purposely threw the sugar and flour everywhere. The shit didn't make no damn sense next thing I know someone knocked on the door. I figured it was the manager of the building. I managed to open the door.

"Say man you got some more of that diesel?"

"Nigga don't you see my door hangin off the hinges?"

"Damn what happen fam?"

Nigga the damn task force just hit a muthafucka. You sure you ain't workin wit them?" I looked at his azz for any form of nervousness.

"Come on now man, how long I been fuckin wit you?"

The cat was one of my regulars so I took the chance.

"Fuck it nigga, come on in" as he walked passed me.

"How much you workin wit?"

"I got 130" he said, fumblin wit his money.

"Hold on" I went over to the couch where I had stuffed the stash. It was dipped in the upper part like where you lay back on, feel me? A cool stash spot, the holice was shook. "Here take all this shit." I doubled him up just to get rid of that shit. I damn near gave him a quarter ounce I felt like I needed to get that shit out of there. I wasn't really scared and I knew he couldn't be settin me up the police had just left that was too fast for them to setup a return sting.

"Damn thanks my nigga. That's why I fucks wit you. You be lookin out."

The next day the landlord told me I had to move. Shit I had no choice I had to get my grind back on. L.P.'s moms was trippin on him now bout hustlin, but shit, I was homeless. I hit the streets and it was do or die. I didn't have time to be scared, feel me? You know that's the best hustla – a broke nigga. I got my paper up and found another apartment close to my school.

CHAPTER 8

By this time L.P.'s mom went to jail and he started staying with me again. One night we was on the block and this girl we knew told us her uncle be fucking with Prince and he got his own studio he was looking for some rappers. The next day we got up with her uncle, Maxx G. We went to this house and in the basement he had keyboards, two drum machines and a mic coming from the ceiling. I had never really been in a studio so I was like "damn."

"So let me hear y'all rap said Maxx G as we stood there amazed.

"What kinda rhyme you wanna hear Jason said, ready with a barrage of wordplay.

"Let me hear y'all freestyle."

Jason started busting hard as fuck, then I came in and did my thang and in like seconds, Maxx G had made a beat. It was our first recording. A song called "What a Brotha know." That shit was hot and niggaz was feeling it, saying we should go and record an album. So we was like "let's grind this paper up and get in the studio knock this album out."

It wasn't four days passed and L.P caught a case on the block, fucked up everything. L.P. was locked down for like 2 months. When he got out it was a surprise cause we thought he was gone for good. During the time he was locked up my homeboy Robdog had moved in with me. Homey look dead on like DJ Quik, real talk.

One day I came to the crib and he was like: "Say cuz, I met this DJ. He stay across the hall."

So we went and saw dude.

"Who is it" Robdog had knocked on the door and I stood there beside him.

"It's Rob from across the hall."

"What's up?"

"Hey man, this my homey wood I was telling you about earlier." I stepped up.

"How you doing man?"

"Alright come on in."

"What's your name man" I asked walking in.

"DJ Mixim". He was a college student at the University of Minnesota a white square dude not from our world but he was cool.

"How long you been djing?" The Cat didn't have no furniture at all, all he had was a gang of records, two turntables and a drum machine.

"About eight years now."

"We looking for a dj for our group the Dope Boyz" That'll be cool, I'd like that."

This was perfect, me and Robdog started hanging out over at his apartment and the next thing we knew L.P. was coming home. It was all good. All we did was record.

Right around this time we met a friend of L.P.'s family who worked at the radio station and thought we was tight. He said that in a few weeks he'd have a situation for us. Like a month later I get a call from dude, his name was DC, Dwayne Carter.

"Say Fleetwood what's happening brotha, how you doing?"

"Look I got a situation if y'all ready."

"Yo that's all we been doing, getting ready, we got some dope shit."

"When can I hear it?"

"Tonight. Right now. Whenever you ready."

"Well look, I got a few meetings then why don't y'all call me and come through."

"Cool."

I called LP and in a few hours we got wit DC and he loved our shit. He was really feeling it. So D.C had an audition set up for us with these cats called Catch 22 – The Marsh Brothers. They'd recently produced The Jets album up in Minnesota and were known for being hot producers. We first met them at DC's house.

"How y'all fellas doing? We done heard a lotta good things about y'all" said the slim brotha.

Both had on cashmere trench coats. One was slim, bald wit glasses, the other kinda stocky wit an afro.

"So DC tells us y'all have a lotta talent."

"Yeah, that's true" L.P. said.

"Well lets hear what y'all working with. Play something."

DC pushed play and we went into attack mode. When the music went off the older brotha looked at me and was like

"So what's your name?"

"They call me Fleetwood."

"How old r u?"

"I'm 26 and I attend music tech."

"So how you like it?"

"It's cool so far."

"Look, I think we can make a lotta money together."

"Most definitely" we said simultaneously.

"Well we need y'all to meet us at 1339 Evans at 3 PM Thursday. Today is Monday so that'll give y'all 3 days to work out any kinks."

"Cool we'll be there" I said.

"We bout to make y'all super rich" L.P. said wit strong belief, they looked at us.

"We all gonna get rich together."

Something didn't seem right but I figured maybe I was just paranoid. When the day came we walked in the studio, Flyght Tyme. I didn't know at the time, but they had just recorded Janet Jackson's Rhythm Nation album there. I saw the Platinum plaques on the wall and was like "we getting close."

We started freestylin and they were like "y'all like this beat?"

"Yeah it's cool" I said.

"Well write something bout your favorite girl in the world for it."

"How many bars you want" I said with a curious look.

I had learned about bars and measures in school. They kinda look-ed at me like "nigga you a little too smart for your own good." Then they gave us a contract.

"Take this and look it over and in a couple days we'll get back together and take care of the paper work so we can start doing real business together."

"That sound cool to me" Jason said.

"What bout you Fleetwood" they asked staring blankly.

I just really wanna read through the paperwork and make sure it's in the best interest of everyone" I said wit a straight face.

"Well it's all business Fleetwood you'll learn in this game it's better to have a little of something than a whole lot of nothin."

That shit sounded good but I wasn't rappin for free for nobody. If I did it would be for the homeys on the block.

"I understand." Fuck what they was talking bout. We exchanged hand shakes and they said they'd get back with us in a couple of days.

I had just switched schools and instead of electronic engineering at Brown Institute I was at Music Tech for Audio Engineering. The next day I took the contract to a lawyer at my school who'd worked in the business.

"How you doing Mr. Leighberg" I said, stickin my head into his doorway.

"Mr. Rebel rapper himself. What you up to?" he said with a smile. I was known in the school to be very vocal wit my opinions.

"You remember I told you that I had a group called 'The dope boys' and that we had some people interested in us."

"Oh yes, I do remember you mentioning that."

"Well they offered us a contract last night and told us to look it over and bring it back."

"Is that right? Do you have it with you?"

"Most definitely right here."

I handed him the contract and he scanned through it, page after page. His eyebrow kept raisin and he kept checkin things on the contract wit his marker.

"Well young man, first of all this is your average production deal, which in all actuality is a slave contract. Basically you give up all your publishing. It's an exclusive deal, meaning they own the rights to every aspect of income you can receive. Also they own creative control, meaning they decide what type of music you make. They also own your power of attorney, meaning they sign any legal documents needed with your name on it. Basically they own you for the amount of albums you sign for."

"Damn so what do we get out of the deal?"

"Well you get to look like superstars. If you lucky and you make a hit record, you'll have a little more negotiation power because your music is a hit and if you decide not to record any more music or tour then the label will lose money. And the label's whole reason for existing is to make a profit. Understand?"

"So what would you suggest I do?"

"Ask yourself do you want the fame or the change. If you want the change take this contract back and where I've highlighted the area's ask them would they be willing to negotiate? If you just want the fame sign it."

"Now you know I ain't bout to do that sir."

"Yeah I pretty much figured that rebel."

"I definitely appreciate you looking out like you did, for real."

"Don't mention it. Just remember to always get someone to look over a contract before you sign it."

"I understand."

I was hot as I walked out of his office, my street instincts kickin in. These marks was trying to play me and basically pimp us. Well I wasn't nobody's ho, believe that. Along with the music classes I also took classes on the business of music. I was well aware of what Mr.

Leighberg was speaking on but this was the first time I had actually witnessed how scandalous the music business was.

I always remembered what Harry O told me.

"The game is based on exploitation. Owning your masters will prevent you from being exploited."

I'd seen documentary after documentary about former superstars now back to being regular joes. The whole entertainment business is based on finding some young kid, blinded by the lights of stardom who wants so bad to be on TV, to wear the jewelry, drive the cars, have all the girls and all the money. In all actuality the average recording artist is strugglin. That's why most have drug and alcohol problems, that stress of knowing someone is screwing you and you can't do shit about it. You signed a deal with them and can't even get your folks out the projects.

The few who do have money are the ones who came right out the gate wit hit records – Nelly, Emenim, 50, and were able to renagotiate a better deal, start their own boutique label under a major wit distribution. Then they can renegotiate their deal, where they now receive a good portion of their publishing wit a high point rating on their records. The other people getting money are the independent label owners. They finance their own situations, get to retain ownership of their masters, the songs, and the publishing.

In a record deal, publishing is the key. You get paid quicker off your publishing than your record. Publishing comes from your airplay, radio spins, merchandising, things like that. Usually an artists will only get an advance and you actually only get paid quarterly from record sales. And that's after the label has deducted the cost of your expenses which include the video, clothes, hair stylist, dinners, hotels, weed. Basically everything.

Basically a record company is like a bank, they loan you the money to get your record out. But to be on a competitive level with other rappers, to be able to do that and have a quality sound takes money – one to two million easy. Most homeys in the hood don't have that. You can start small in your region, build yourself up like Too $hort,

E-40, Master P etc., but that's also why you find so many rappers in jail, they were hustling to pay for their dream. Or you see a lotta the little homeys signing them "neighborhood nigga deals": fucking wit a balla type shit. Them niggaz so usta seeing a quick profit that they really ain't no different from them scandalous azz labels. They gangsta wit it. That's all most label heads are – corporate gangstas, extorting niggaz outta their creative works.

So there it was. My second lesson in the realities of the music business. I couldn't wait to see these scandalous muthafuckas to tell them I knew what they were up to. Two days later we had dinner with Catch 22.

"Fleetwood, Jason how's my favorite rappers doing?" said one wit a slick smile.

"Oh we straight, we straight" said Jason.

"I'm cool brotha how you doing" I said looking him dead in his eyes. I informed them that we had checked into their paperwork and people had advised us about the contract. They didn't like that shit at all and after that dinner, the calls from them stop coming. It was now 1991 and L.P was kinda hot saying we should have just signed but we wasn't gonna get shit but our pictures on an album cover while we get them rich. As time went by we kept recording.

Around this time I met Jabo and Major Damage, aspiring rap stars from my school. We began to hang out and record together so eventually we decided to form our own label. We formed Double Up Productions and the next week we threw a rap contest. We signed this group 'Soul Aspect'

My partners TLO and Tech and this dude named the Outkast. I had my homey Bob Blakey running the company wit me. We were doing shows, getting a buzz and everything was cool. Shit was going good.

We did our first show wit E-40 and the Click and I was hella excited. 40 was from the bay holding it down. At the time he had the song out Captain Sav'em and I'll neva forget, before the show, chillin with him, B-legit, Suga-T, D SHOT and JR RIDER who was playing for the Timberwolves at the time. I asked 40 water for some advice and he told me – "Don't neva give up and don't neva hate on nobody." I neva forgot that.

Later on in life I ran into B-legit and we chopped it up at Off Planet Studios in Cali.

Next thing I know I get a call. L.P. has caught another case. This time they wasn't letting him go. They were sending him to Glen Mills home for boys for up to a year. I couldn't believe it. so I kept going to school and hustlin.

We were still recording at my school and at Tangle Town Studios with this dude William Winfield. Sometimes they'd let L.P. get home passes so we'd go and record him.

This one night I was on the block, getting some money and this female I knew wanted something. I went up into this spot and on the way out these niggaz came out this room and upped a pistol on me. There was a big window in the hallway and I thought them niggaz was bout to shoot me, so I went through the window. I was like two floors up and landed on the side of my face on a fence. I blacked out, wit like 20 grams of crack in my draws.

I woke up the next morning in the hospital, handcuffed to a bed. Luckily they hadn't tested the dope yet and at that point it was no charges against me, so I was like – "What y'all holding me for?"

They uncuffed me, I got dressed and bailed, wit my head all fucked up on the side. I went to the crib and chilled for like 3 days. Eventually I knew I would have to take care of the situation that had landed me in the hospital. It wasn't hard to find out the ones responsible and what had to be done had to be done or I couldn't come back on the block. But that shit led to more beef. Now I'm strapped everyday, ridin round with a pistol and a sawed off. TLO joined the Dope Boyz and we kept recording whenever L.P. would come home. By now we were calling ourselves B-double-S (Born Suspect Section.)

We was almost ready to release our first EP "No Time to Sleep" and was just waiting on L.P. to finish his last two months. I really had stayed off the block due to so much beef and was tryin to get this music shit in order and finish school. I was just a few months from graduation. I was coming from the studio one night I had just dropped TLO off when the police pulled me over. I had a license and the pistol was tucked so I wasn't trippin. The next thing I knew they had guns drawn tellin me to get out the car. I had a warrant for possession of cocaine wit intent to distribute. That hospital shit had come back to haunt me.

CHAPTER 9

2000 miles from home, in jail again and lookin at goin to the pen. My homey Dee from Gary, Indiana usta come and see a nigga. That was some real shit and to this day that's my homey. I stayed locked down like a month. Finally, my nigga Major Damage got the funds together and my homey Jabo asked his folks to put up their house for security and they let a nigga out. That was some real shit Jabo folks did, I had really only known the brotha less than a year.

I was out now but it was all bad. I had to take extra courses to graduate because I missed so much. Bills were backed up so I had to hit the block to get my shit right. And plus I had a case, a dead to rights case. It was 1992 and once again my life was unraveling.

I had finally got my bills in order when I got a phone call from my lawyer.

"How you doin Mr. Bowden?"

"I'm cool Mr. Stockdale. What's up?"

"Well I did the best I could. With your past record the best I could get you was 90 months."

"90 months? Fuck n'all. that's damn near 7 years!"

"Well they found prior convictions of the same charge."

"Yo, that's some bullshit! I only got two charges in California!"

"Let me check it out and call you back."

I sat on my couch wit the air conditioning blowin. My azz fell into a deep daze and all of a sudden I hear the phone ring.

"Hello?"

"Mr. Bowden you where correct you only had two convictions."

"I told ya. So what they talkin bout now?"

"I talked to the D.A. and he's willin to drop 30 month off the original offer."

"So you talkin bout 60 months, fuck n'all."

"Look son, you're in a lotta trouble. You ain't gonna win in court, you gotta ride this out."

"I feel ya. Let me think on it and get back to you in a few days."

Shitted, they found crack on me in the hospital, they had me dead to rights. I had like 3 months before my court date but it wasn't no way I was gonna win in court during a trial. L.P. was comin home next week but I was bout to go in. It was December of 1992 and it felt like I was waitin to be executed.

L.P. came home, got back in school and basically just tried to stay free. We kept makin music but it wasn't really the same. I still remember on like ten different occasions, sittin in my apartment at night under the NWA, Public Enemy and Good Times posters, callin the bus station and askin when the next bus to Oakland left. But it felt like Cube, Ren, Dre, Easy, Chuck, Flavor and Thelma was all talkin to me, tellin me how much of a coward I would be to run out on Mrs. Sanders.

I walked through my apartment lookin at the few trinkets that where left in my fucked up life. All the hustlin I did, just a few cars outside and some fucked up shit inside. But I couldn't jump bail and have those people tryin to take my homie's mom's house. I couldn't run out when the lady had looked out for me like that. I just couldn't do it. I wasn't built like that. (Big shout out to Mrs. Sanders.)

I woke up one mornin and it was time to go to court and turn myself in. I looked around my apartment. I had pawned and sold most of my shit to get outta jail and the livin room looked damn near like it did when I moved in. It felt like I was goin to my death even

though I had been in the county hella times in Cali. But I had never
volunteered to let them lock me up. My homeboy Bob Blakey took
me to court. He was doin my verses on the songs now at shows to
help keep things goin. I was standing in a small courtroom wit no one
but the D.A., my lawyer, the court stenographer, my family and some
niggaz in handcuffs behind a plastic petition. I stood there, lookin at
this judge, hopin like hell he'd change his mind.

"All rise. Honorable Judge Milton Powell presiding. Courtroom 45,
docket number 62, everyone raise you right hand." Then the judge
asked me all that usual bullshit they ask you before they lock you
up.

"State attorney has a plea of guilty been reached in this case" the
judge asked. Man he already knew. Them muthafuckas be knowin
what's crackin before you come to court. They discuss that shit in
the massage parlor or at their favorite country clubs.

"Yes your honor we've agreed to a 60 month sentence for the case
of Robert Floyd Bowden vs the state of Minnesota" the D.A. said.

"Mr. Stockdale is this correct?" the judge asked my lawyer.

"Yes your honor."

"Mr. Bowden has anyone promised you anything or threatened
you into takin this plea?"

"No sir."

"Raise your right hand."

"The state of Minnesota at this time sentences Mr. Robert Floyd
Bowden to 60 months in the state correctional facility to serve no less
than 45 months" he finished, bangin his mallet on the wood. I looked
at the door, thinkin "run", but being on the 6th floor, I wasn't bout
to get away. I looked back at the homeys one last time as they led
me into the back room. Within an hour I was in county blues, playin
chess and waitin on the next Grey Goose. They said I'd probably be
outta there in two weeks. Next thing I knew they were callin my
name. "Bowden, roll it up. Your ride's here."

"What you talkin bout man?"

"Roll your shit up it's time to go to the big house" he said it wit a smile, like I was supposed to be terrified.

"Yo I just came from court it must be a mistake or something."

"It's no mistake get your shit and come on!"

I gathered what little I had. In a very short time I'd be entering a prison complex for a five year stay. As the bus pulled into Still Water State Prison I had a flashback of that big azz castle in Lompoc. All that damn barbwire everywhere, the gun tower and the building. It looked like it had been there since Abe Lincoln was in the White House. They brought us in, took us through the usual look up your azz type shit, then marched us to this area of the prison they said was orientation but was really the damn hole. Here we go wit this shit again. As soon as I walked in the muthafucka someone called my name.

"Fleetwood what up folks."

"Muthafuckin Kansas City! What it is my nigga?" It was this nigga that used to run for me on the streets. I was happy as hell to see him, muthafucka looked like the hulk, leanin over that rail on the upper tier. I got settled in and me and Kansas City kicked it. Nigga had swollen up like bee's had stung him.

"Look my nigga, you took care of me out on them streets and ain't nah nigga in here bout to fuck wit you in this joint" he said sneering.

"Oh you know I ain't worried bout no shit like that KC, I holds mine."

"Yeah my nigga that's why I got mad love and respect for you, cause you a soulja. But look, I work in the kitchen, so whatever you need let me know."

"Cool my nigga, I will."

I wasn't really worried bout nobody fuckin wit me. Folks was deep in that bitch, plus I was prepared to hold my own regardless of how shit went down. Bout two weeks passed and one mornin I was in my cell readin and this heavy set dude came in.

"Excuse me, are you Robert Bowden?"

"Yeah what's happenin man?" I lowered my Murdadog magazine.

"My name is Mike Lyon and I'm from the pre-release program.

According to our records it shows that you are eligible for a six month Boot Camp program."

"What are you talkin bout, Boot Camp?" I asked, risin up.

"It's an alternate program to prison. A boot camp where you can go for six months, then you do 6 months of supervised parole, then you're on regular parole."

"So you sayin I can go to this for 6 months, then hit the streets?"

"Yes you can Mr. Bowden."

"What's the catch though? This shit sound too good to be true."

"Well if you don't complete the program at the boot camp or your 6 months of intensive parole, none of the time will count. It'll be all dead time and you'll return to prison to start your time all over wit no credit from the program."

"Damn I knew it was something to it." But I felt like shit, what I got to lose? If they gonna let me out, I'm goin for it." Within 3 days I was on my way to the camp. When the prison guards came to get us they were hella cool.

"So how are y'all doin today?" A female guard asked on the way to the camp.

"I'm cool, " I said.

"I'm just glad to be out of there" said this Mexican dude.

"So what have y'all heard bout the place?"

"My homey told me it's what you make out of it. I ain't worried though, whatever it is I'mma do it and go home" I said wit conviction.

"You seemed to be determined to make it through."

"Ma'am no disrespect intended but it can't be no worser than the streets in my hood."

"Well it might be a different kind of warfare though."

"What you mean?"

"Let's just say the physical aspect counts but it's more mental than anything. You have to have a strong mind to last."

"My spirit strong so my mind strong, feel me?"

I kicked back, meditated and prepared for the worst while hopin for the best. I could hear her conversatin wit the other convicts but

I kept quite. As soon as we pulled into the boot camp, man these muthafucka's flipped. They started yellin and shit for us to get out the van and line up. I looked around and there was no fences. I had no idea where the fuck I was.

As we stood in line wit bad breath punks all in our faces I noticed it was a bunch of people dressed in khaki's doin all kinds of yard work. Some were joggin, singin songs and shit. I realized right then I had got myself into a real twist. They explained all the rules: we would be required to run 3 miles at 5AM, do 100 push ups and sit-ups, then go back shower and prepare for breakfast. After that would be an inspection, then work detail, then lunch, more work detail, then dinner and more work detail. Come in at 8 PM and lights out by 9. during the hours of 8–9PM, we where supposed to get our clothes ironed and boots gleamin and shinin for the next day. This was Monday through Saturday. Sunday was free if you earned it, and you weren't allowed any visitin or phone calls for 60 days depending upon your score that you received daily.

This point system also determined your level. Red was entry, blue was next and brown was your last 60 days. Oh yeah I forgot to mention, this was one of the few co-ed facilities in the nation. Even though the program was six months you could be there a lot longer if you were set back. I had met this one cat who had been there seven months and he still was in a red hat so I knew I had to play their game to go home.

"Yo homey how long you been here" I asked him. I knew he hadn't come in wit us but he had on the same color hat, plus the word had got back to us that he was the fuck up at the complex.

"On some real shit these KKK members done had me up here damn near ten months and I'm still in a red hat."

"Damn brotha what you do?"

"I'm not bout havin them to try change me just cause I don't wanna stand a certain way or cause I curse or can't run as many miles as they want me to. They keep sayin I'm not gettin enough points to advance. The same ol bullshit every time."

"So when you lookin at goin home?"

"Man I don't even know."

'Well what if you stay here a year then they send you back? That's gonna be ugly homey."

"Yeah I feel ya."

"Shit I'mma do whatever I gotta do to get outta here."

"Alright homey, I'm bout to get ready fo inspection what's your name though?"

"Bowden." Up there you had to go by your last name.

"Demery. They call me Demery."

"Alright be cool homey, I'll holla."

At that moment I made up my mind I wasn't bout to play myself like that. It was all bout reverse psychology wit these people. I knew I had to stay spiritually strong at all times and stay very close to God. I had grabbed the Holy Q'uran and stayed deep into it every chance I got. during my short stay in Stillwater prison I'd been talkin wit the O.G Muslim and I was feelin what he was sayin bout Islam. Even though I was raised as a Baptist it always confused me. Islam taught me more bout being a Black man in America. So I embraced it and at the time I remember how he had said that only his faith had allowed him to do 12 years at that point. So I felt this would be my strength to get through this shit.

Within a month I wrote my little sista Attica in Cali to send help! I told her to contact the Urban League, NAACP, Jesse Jackson, anybody, somebody to let them know these Nazi's in these mountains was tryin to kill us! To this day she gets a big laugh outta that letter. But the shit wasn't funny, I was dead serious. These muthafucka's had us runnin in snow, rain, whatever. Diggin holes then filling the same hole back up. Then we would come in and all our shit would be thrown on the floor wit them sayin we didn't pass the inspection. They did plenty of shit just to fuck wit a nigga.

One day I stopped brushing my teeth. I had got tired of them hollering and yellin at me all in my face. So after like 3 weeks – "Bowden, damn son your personal hygiene is completely out of order" said the sergeant, disgusted.

"Sir! Yes sir!" I said as forceful as I could, pushin as much bad breath as I could out of my mouth. The sergeant backed up hella fast and shook his head. We all got a good laugh outta that. That little joke seemed to get us through the next month. We had made our first 2 months when at like 2 in the mornin we were woke up. Someone had escaped. Two crazy azz white boys had stole the van and bailed. A week later they were caught but the place was on high alert for the next 90 days.

I awoke one mornin ready to go to exercise and realized I was 2 weeks away from the streets. Finally this shit was comin to an end. during my stay at this boot camp I continued to write songs whenever I could. During my last 2 weeks I just tried to go over my plan for the free world as much as possible. Our day finally came and it was time to leave this dreaded place, I had did a lotta time in my life but this shit was by far the hardest I had ever did. Due to the fact I wasn't from Minnesota and had no family or address, these mothafuckas sent me to the halfway house until I could get an apartment.

"Mr. Bowden you do realize this is only a temporary housing situation for you until you find your own housing?"

"Yeah I do understand man."

"Do I detect a bit of a attitude?"

"What you talkin bout man?"

"My name is Mr. Williams, not man."

"Mr. Williams what are you talkin bout? I only responded to what you said."

I knew right then this dude had on panties, so I had to be cool in all aspects of dealin wit him.

CHAPTER 10

Right when I walked in the halfway house they introduced me to my counselor.

"Close the door boy."

"What?"

"I said close the door! Do you have a problem wit that? Cause if so you can go back to prison, it's certain things I don't tolerate here and the number one is back talk from any convict."

" I'm not a convict, I'm an ex convict."

"I see already we gonna have a problem wit you."

"Look dude I don't wanna be here like you don't want me to be here" I told him.

"Yeah you right. I think guys like you would be better off in prison rottin doin your time. All these new programs are ridiculous."

"Is that right? Imagine that."

"Well here are the rules. Break any one and I will send you back to prison faster than you can blink boy."

"I'll keep that in mind buddy."

"My name is Mr. James."

"Well Mr. James I know you don't like me and I want you to know I don't like you, so at least it ain't no fakin. Do yours to get me locked back up and I'll do mine to stay free."

"Get out of my office wit that prison jargon boy."

I knew he was a racist azzhole usin his position to get back at muthafuckas like me who had punked him all his life. The first night I was there L.P. and TLO came by. L.P. had plugged in wit some Chicago folks and the little nigga was havin it. TLO was right on his side and had came up wit a new car and shit.

"Damn y'all niggaz ballin huh?"

"Wood you know we got to get it while it's good" said Jason smilin from ear to ear.

"We ain't doin too much Fleet, just eatin brotha."

"Shit it look like y'all doin more than eatin my nigga."

"Wood you alright bro? You need some money?"

"Hell yeah, I need to get the fuck outta here get me an apartment."

"I can hit you wit something. You ain't got to touch it and come up. Get the fuck outta this place in a few days, feel me?"

"Man I ain't even tryin to go that route right now fam. I'mma try shit the other way feel me?"

"Yeah wood, but if you change your mind get at me."

"Cool my nigga, cool."

"Yo here go something to keep the pocket warm bro."

"Thanks my nigga."

"I got you, don't trip."

"So what's up wit the music?"

"Wood that's what we grindin fo, studio time. You remember you usta pay for all the shit. Let me handle that my nigga."

"You grown now Jason, all I can do is tell you what I been through and hope you don't go through the same shit lil homey. Feel me?"

"I feel ya wood but I got this shit."

"Y'all be careful, call me tomorrow fam."

As I watched my lil homey walk away I reminisced back to when I had first met him on Pillsbury at his cousin house. Time had passed fast, it definitely don't wait on nobody. I knew we where hot together and I knew I had to stay free. Before they left we decided to finish up the "No Time to Sleep" E.P. as soon as possible. I was stuck on being straight and not hustlin at all. I got a job in this meat company cuttin meat. The shit used to gross me the fuck out, but I was willin to do whatever it took to stay outta jail cause I knew they couldn't wait to violate me.

Me and the punk azz counselor at the halfway house had got into like four or five arguments and he was tryin bad to get me sent back. I had been out now two months, I only had four more to go on this intensive shit and I would then be on regular parole, but this mutha-fuckin counselor at this halfway house kept fuckin wit me. I had a little money stacked, not enough for an apartment, but I got a room in a boardin house. It was cool, a lot bigger than the cells I'd seen. The 1940 pictures on the walls and the thin carpet gave it a feel of home and it smelled of apples.

That same night I moved in I called my homey Brickhead and he told me an old breezy of mine had been askin bout me. I persuaded my homey to see if he could find her. Forty five minutes later it was a knock at the door.

"Who is it" I said hopin like fuck it was my nigga Brickhead wit Charlotte.

She answered in that one in a million voice "It's Charlotte. Is Fleet-wood here?" Unmistakably familiar.

"Hey baby girl. Damn you a sight for sore eyes, you look good as fuck." She walked passed me into the room, all eyes was on that bubble gum azz of hers, hand all in my pocket tryin to conceal my excitement.

"Give me a hug baby" she said.

I opened my arms, embracin her.

"Fleetwood you feel good in my arms daddy."

"Why you didn't write the whole time I was down?"

"I was mad at you for leavin me out here by myself."

"It's cool mama. I would probably have went crazy tryin to do time wit you on my mind."

"So you didn't never think bout me" she said lookin deep down in my eyes.

"I thought bout you quite often but I knew it was wise for me to stay inside that world and outta the free world, you feel me?"

"Well come mere and get all inside this world" she said layin back on the bed and openin her legs wide. Her skirt slid up her thighs and I slid deep inside her.

"Look daddy," she said. "I want to help you get back on your feet. I hit a little lick and I got something for you."

"Something like what?"

"It's a surprise Fleetwood."

"Now you know I don't like no damn surprises."

"Dang okay, I got some weed I'mma give you"

"Some weed? How much?"

Now look how fast the devil works. I had just told my little homey I was gonna chill but here I was bout to start slangin weed, tryin to convince myself that it was only weed.

"I got some pounds. I'll hit you wit a few so you can get back like you usta. I wanna see you shine."

'Shit I'm glad you feel that way, so when we gonna make this situation reality?"

"Tomorrow baby, tomorrow. Now come here wit your sexy black azz."

The next day she brought me 4 pounds of weed.

When she said it I thought she was bullshittin, but here she was sittin in my room tellin me how she wanted to see me havin thangs again.

"Here you go daddy, get what you got comin and you don't owe me nothin."

"Thank you lil mama I ain't gonna never forget this."

That shit lasted bout two weeks and even though all the homeys would come and fuck wit me the money wasn't comin fast enough. I was like "if they catch me wit this weed I'm goin back, so I might as well get me some hard and come up for real." Only one problem, I was gettin tested every three days plus I couldn't be on the block at all. But until I got my clientèle up I would have to be on the block.

I had to find someone I could half way trust to move this shit for me. I had a homey Randall that wasn't doin that good. He was from the hood and I knew he was a go getter that just didn't have a plug. I called him.

"Hello" a familiar voice said on the other end of the phone.

"Ay Randall this Fleetwood. I need to holla at you homey."

"Damn what up Fleet they told me you was out. What's on your mind?" You could hear the excitement in his voice.

"Look you know I don't like talkin on no phones. When can you meet at the park on Franklin?"

"I'll be there in a hour"

"Cool I'll see you there."

An hour later Randall walks towards me as I sit on a bench readin the mornin paper.

"What up folks" I say.

"Damn fam you done got hella swoll" he said laughin.

"So sitdown, this what I wanted to holla at you bout."

"What's up?"

"Look you know I just got out and I can't touch nothin but I got the plug. I need to fuck wit someone I can trust who won't be bullshit. We can get some money real talk."

"Wood you know damn well you can trust me and I'm starvin like fuck. This right on time."

I called L.P.

"Jason I need to holla at you. I'm ready."

"I thought you wasn't fuckin around? I knew you was gonna change your mind wood. You taught me how to grind."

"I'm just tired of this boardin room shit."

That night me and Randall was choppin down a fresh ounce. In two weeks we was up to four zips and I had an apartment, fresh furniture and a gang of gear. A few weeks passed and it was goin good, but I was still on that intensive boot camp shit. I was supposed to be workin 40 hours, but I was on the block gettin money. Plus I wasn't suppose to use drugs, have a beeper or use a cell phone. I was gettin tired of that shit. I'd been missing work, and one mornin I heard someone knockin at the door. Randall and his breezy was on the couch sleep. My breezy was in the bedroom. Liquor bottles, cell phones and beepers was everywhere. My P.O. walks in.

"Mr. Bowden you realize you are in violation of your supervised parole?"

"How is that sir" I asked, as straight faced as I could.

"It's clearly stated that no cellular phones or pagers are to be in your possession at anytime."

"Those are my friends, not mine."

"But this is your home, and what bout the alcoholic beverages and paraphernalia I see?"

"I don't have no idea what you are talkin bout, it's just a misunderstanding that's all."

"Well I think you need to come down to the office and explain it to us."

"No problem."

I already knew what that meant. They was gonna lock the doors when I got down there. I didn't go and I was gettin my shit packed. I was on my way back home to Cali. As I'm comin out my apartment I hear that all too familiar sound.

"Freeze get your muthafuckin hands up! Get your muthafuckin hands up!" the task force was screamin at the top of their voices.

The police had the building surrounded, waitin on a nigga. It was all bad. They found 3 racks on me and I had a quarter ounce stuffed. On the way to the station they picked up someone else. I tried to pass the dope to this nigga in the back of the car but the shit dropped down the seat. When they took us out the car they pulled the seat out and their eyes lit up, like "yeah muthafucka we got you now."

So here I was sittin in the bullpen in the county wit a new charge. Plus I knew I was violated and then it finally hit me. I had did damn near a year, none of the time was gonna count because I hadn't finish their punk azz program and I only had like 35 more days to go. They kept a nigga in the county jail like a month, then shipped me to the county workhouse. I had five years of dead time waitin on me. I felt like my world had ended.

L.P and TLO had finished the EP and was doin their thang. One day I call L.P and he was like they were bout to go open up for Scarface, Bone Thugs n' Harmony and Fifth Ward Boys. My damn heart bout dropped out. I couldn't believe this shit. I was locked down and the dream we all had worked on was finally comin true. I was depressed as hell. The next night I was layin in my bunk listenin to the radio and boom, I heard DC Djin. He was talkin bout me.

"This song right here we sending this out to our homeboy Fleetwood in the workhouse. Fleet you keep your head up partna we got you." Then he played our single, "Inna City Soulja." The feelin you get hearing your song on the radio is very hard to describe. It's like a orgasm. Damn near all the niggaz in the tier was goin crazy like "nigga that's you!" It felt good but at the same time I was smilin to keep from cryin.

A few weeks went by and L.P and TLO were bout to do a show wit Notorious BIG, Junior Mafia and DA Brat. The reality had sat in they was bout to blow without me. They promised that it would always be a spot for me and that no one could take that. That shit sounded good but it wasn't no guarantee that I was gonna make it out of that prison. From doin time before I knew it was a no no to be all into feelings inside them walls but I had a breezy that swore she was gonna hold me down. I guess I let my guard down or whatever and really started believin the shit she was sayin. I got more attached to her every day wit the letters, visits and calls. One mornin I called her.

"Hello" a young female said on the other end.

"May I speak to Shelly?"

"Who's callin" she asked.

"Fleetwood."

"Hold on for a minute"

"Yeah hello" she answered.

"What's wrong wit you?"

"Nothin."

"Why you sound like that?"

"Like what? I just said hello. Shit."

"You know lately I been detectin an attitude wit you every time I call."

'I don't be havin no attitude. You the one be trippin like you my daddy or something."

"Oh now you brand new on a nigga? Man look, just send me my loot and we gonna cut ties. That way we won't need to conversate for nothin."

"Nigga that money gone."

"You spent my money huh?"

"Hell yeah I spent it now what bitch azz nigga? Fuck you, my uncle gonna holla at you too. He in there."

'Look tramp you gonna get burnt playin wit fire don't you know that?"

"Nigga you ain't gon do shit and you know what? I'm tired of your azz. Don't call my house no more" she said, addin "if you do I'll file charges against your punk azz" before she hung up.

Chow time was in thirty minutes so me, Tyson and Bunk – a young, wild, crip nigga facin like ten who could rhyme his azz off – was chillin.

"Fleet you need to chill big homey read or do some push ups, play some chess or something. I can see the stress all in your face."

"I'm cool lil homey, just gotta keep my head inside this fence."

"You gotta stay off that phone Fleet you know better than that. You told me bout that phone."

"Bunk I ain't callin that trick no more. I'm through wit that lazy azz broad."

"That easier said than done homey."

Right when he said that the chow bell rang. We all headed for the chow hall and I got in line but I'd left my radio on my bed so I dipped back to get it right quick. When I came back, this big azz hillbilly was like "go to the back" but I ignored him. Then he got up on me and my instincts kicked in. I stole on him and the next thing I know he was on the floor, bleedin bad from the nose and screamin "he hit me! He hit me!" When the guards came he pointed me out.

"What happened to that man?"

"I have no idea officer"

"Why's he screamin you hit him?"

"He confused. I didn't hit him."

"Well we gonna have to take you to the hole until we finish the investigation."

"This some bullshit man."

"If you didn't do nothin you don't have nothin to worry bout, now do ya?"

"Like y'all gonna believe me."

They took me to the hole, the first night in there I felt like I couldn't breath but as the days passed it got a little easier. Bunk and Tyson would send me shit and I had folks in the kitchen that made sure my trays were doubled up. Never in my life had I been in such a hurry to go to court, but I was ready to get this shit over wit. Even though I had adjusted, being in the hole was fucked up: locked down 23 hours a day and comin out for just one hour will eventually make a nigga feel like an animal. They'd given me one hundred and twenty days in the hole and two months had passed. Tyson got out and I was happy for him and sad too. That's how it is wit the homeys leavin you behind in jail.

I was just layin down readin one day when I heard Bunk yellin "Hell n'all.! Fuck n'all!" He was on the phone screamin and the next thing I know he was at my bars.

"Fleetwood them muthafuckas killed Tyson homey! They killed him for nothin" he said wit tears in his eyes.

I was confused "What you talkin bout Bunk? Slow down."

"I just got off the phone wit my cousin. They usta run together before Tyson got locked up."

"What he say happen?"

"He said some niggaz tried to rob him and he wasn't goin for it so they shot him."

"That's what it's bout now my nigga. These niggaz done turned robbery into a neighborhood hustle."

I couldn't believe this shit here my nigga had been tryin to bail out for months and when he finally got the money and property up to get out he didn't even live a month. It was like a nigga was safer in jail. For the next few weeks shit was real quiet in the tiers. Bunk got sent to the hole and he gotten me back into writin by freestylin' every night. I told him "look lil homey, if you get that time, the best thing you can do is read and write everyday. It'll keep your mind strong in that monster."

"That's what I'mma do big homey watch when I come home I'mma have so many rhymes they ain't gonna be able to fuck wit me."

"I believe you my nigga, I believe you." Now it's ten years later and we still talk. He's now known as Young Pluky and he's got over 1,000 rhymes.

Finally my day came to go to court. It wasn't even a courtroom, just some little side room. As I walked in they looked at me hella funny. That punk from the halfway house was there.

"Mr. Bowden could you have a seat please."

I sat down, across from the arbitrator and lookin dead at him.

"Do you realize how many violations you have concernin the CIIP program?"

"I felt like I was doin what I was supposed to do" I told him.

"Well unfortunately, you are were wrong Mr. Bowden. I must inform you that you have failed the program and will be sent back to a state correctional facility immediately. Hopefully things will work out for you when you do get out five years from now." The shit took like 5 minutes. They could have done this shit months ago, but you know the system. It's all profit for them either way and they like to play games wit a nigga. I never went back to the workhouse. After the revocation hearing they took me to the holdin cell and within a few hours I was on a van headed to another prison.

CHAPTER 11

As we pulled in I noticed it didn't look like a castle but it still had the fences, hella barbwire and plenty of hillbillies wit shotguns. I stepped off the van and saw a big sign that read "Welcome to Lino Lakes Correctional Facility." Once again I didn't know where the fuck I was or how long I was gonna be there. One thing I did know: I wasn't bout to see the streets no time soon, so I got settled in. It was 1993, my out date was Oct 16, 1997.

The place kinda reminded me of a college campus, a medium security joint similar to the minimum camp at the feds, but it had fences. A few weeks passed and I got my TV and enrolled in a computer class. One day I met this youngsta liftin weights.

"What's up lil homey how you doin?"

"I'm cool big cuz'n, where you from?"

"I'm from Cali but I been stayin in Minneapolis."

"Yeah, I'm from the Rollin Sixties Crips cuz"

"How long you been down" I asked him.

"Bout two years. I'm bout to get out in a year and put me a album out and blow the fuck up."

"You be rappin or singin or something?"

"I be rappin cuz. They got a studio in the next room. I've recorded like four songs in there already."

"They got a studio in where" I asked?

"In there"

'You bullshittin cuz, a real studio?"

"They got enough shit where you can record a song wit a good sound."

"Yo lets check it out."

"Cool. Lets finish a few more sets then we can go over there."

"What's your name by the way big homey? They call me Cashflow."

"Yeah they call me Fleetwood lil homey."

They had a mixing board, a mic and a four track recorder. It was a big azz nigga in there wit a keyboard doin his thang. He introduced himself.

"How you doin brotha, my name's Poindexter."

Cashflow told me he was an ex panther who had killed a policeman and was at the end of doin a 20 to life sentence.

"I'm cool brotha my name's Fleetwood and I just pulled up. Cashflow told me bout this studio and I thought he was bullshittin."

"See cuz I wasn't lyin huh" Cashflow said smilin.

"Yeah Cash been in here doin his thang."

"So you know how to run all this equipment?"

"Yeah, I been down here for the last five years. I run this studio. I petitioned for it when I first got here to help keep brothas musical dreams alive."

"That's some real shit big homey."

"So you rap too?"

"Yeah I fucks wit that shit. I had just released a record when I got caught up. I got a group on the streets."

"Is that right?"

"Yes sir."

"Well we don't have a lotta fancy stuff here but I'm willin to help you as much as I can."

"Yo, I appreciate that family. Fo real."

"Yo let's go, it's bout count time" Cashflow said lookin at the clock. "We can come back after count."

"Say Fleetwood let me share something wit you before you leave."

"What's that Poindexter?"

"What I would do if I was you is take this time in my life, how long you said you gonna to be down?"

"Five years homey." For the first time, compared to his 20 to life, it didn't seemed that long.

"I would use this time to study the music business, you should order this book called "All You Need To Know About the Music Business" by Donald Passman. It'll teach you the game."

"I don't know if I mentioned it, but I just graduated from Music Tech for Audio engineering and we also had music business classes."

"Son, you can never learn enough when it comes to this music business."

"No I didn't mean it like that. I appreciate what you tellin me and I'm definitely bout to order that book, fo real."

During count I couldn't wait to come out the room so I could call the homeys. I saw the lights come on in the hallway that meant count was clear. I came out like a horse at the races and headed for the phone. I dialed the number.

Jason's mother answered "Hello Suge may I speak to Jason?"

"Hold on Floyd" she refused to call me Fleetwood.

"Yeah what up man?"

"J dog I need a favor fam."

"What you need wood?"

"It's a book entitled 'All You Need To Know About the Music Business' it's by Donald Passman. I need that."

"That's all?"

"Yeah my nigga that's it."

'Shitted, I thought you really needed something big."

"That is big, it's gonna help further my understanding on the business of music."

"I feel ya. N'all I mean I thought you needed a move or something" he said laughin and I joined in.

"I'mma holla at'cha later."

"Okay my nigga keep your head up."

"Fo sho'."

"Love."

"Love."

Right when I got off the phone I saw this nigga that was in the boot camp wit me, Mark Lewis from Compton. I knew him on the streets he was a PIRU who usta be wit a DAMU I knew name Jr. Lew that's what we called him.

"Say blood what's happenin?"

"Muthafuckin Fleetwood! What you doin here?"

"Shit they violated my azz. I had 30 days to go to regular parole blood."

"They got me wit some coke and a strap. The punk azz parole officer was tryin hard to push for a new case."

"Man Lew can you believe we went through all that boot camp shit just to start over again."

"Ain't that a bitch blood."

"So how long you been here?"

"Bout 3 months goin on 4. I got 3 years and 7 months to go."

"Shit I got 60 months blood, real talk."

As we walked through the yard Lew asked "So Fleetwood, what's up wit your music homey?"

"Man my homey tryin hard to keep the shit goin while I'm in here, so basically all I can do is learn as much as I can bout the business side of it, feel me?"

"You know they got a studio here"

'Yeah I met this crip nigga name Cashflow who took me in there."

"Yeah that's my boy's nephew. Cashflow solid."

"I figured I go back in there and fuck wit the shit but I don't know blood. On one hand it's cool and on the other hand it's like 'why the fuck did this shit happen?"

"Wood, GOD got his reasons, one day you'll understand why."

"Yeah I feel ya."

"Yo let me introduce you to my homeboy. Raheem be up in that studio flowin. The boy raw."

"Rah this my partna from Oakland, Fleetwood. I know him from the block plus we was in that boot camp together."

Raheem was sittin on a bench and he slid off one of his earphones.

"What up homey Raheem"

"Fleetwood. Family."

Raheem was from Rockford, IL. A real nigga who got caught up in a raid and wit some weight was involved. Now he had seven years to do. He had got caught wit some work and they violated him. We laughed bout the boot camp days then went and got some weed and walked the yard.

"So you from Cali, huh?" Raheem asked.

"Yeah the bay man."

"You usta fuck wit Too $hort?"

"Not really like that but we was raised off $hort and E-40 all day."

"So you be rappin?"

"Yeah I fucks wit that shit" I said.

"I know Lew wouldn't have mentioned you unless you be doin your thang."

"Yeah I had a little situation on the streets. Let me hear something."

The nigga start rhymin and I thought Wu-Tang was in the building. The nigga had that style mastered. "The lil homey Cashflow, I met him earlier, he tight. You know him?"

"Yeah I seen him in the studio one day, his shit is hot."

"Let me spit something for you." I said some of that shit off "Inna City Soulja." The niggaz mouth fell open.

"Looka here Fleetwood, we all three need to just get together and go in there and form us a group and make an album in here."

'Shit I'm wit it. I'll holla at Cashflow when I get back to the cottage."

I could tell Raheem was amped bout the idea. That's how hip hop is. It'll give you life when you feel hopeless. It has it's own fire. Hip hop has always been the voice of the havenots venting their frustrations or celebrating the accomplishments many thought never could be made.

So now here we were in prison, three convicts from three different hoods bout to start venting life from the inside lookin out. Later that night we all three got together and decided on the name "Maximum Security." Around eight or nine months passed and we had 15 songs. wit the limited equipment we did them wit, the shit sounded cool. I usta call the crib and let the homeys hear some of the shit and they couldn't believe I was makin music like that in the penitentiary.

My daily routine consisted of weight liftin, watchin BET, writin and readin that music business book which I enjoyed the most. It amazed me how the music business really worked. I learned bout points, cross collatterization, publishing, copyrights how to read a contract and the most important thing was I learned that the music business was a game of exploitation. Pimpin' and gettin pimped. This was show business. If you didn't know nobody was gonna tell you. 90% business and 10% show. The months disappeared and every time I would call home all I heard bout was how TLO and L.P. was rollin. I just told them to be careful and keep that music shit goin. Me, Cashflow and Raheem kept recording.

It was early '95 now and I had less than 2 years left but the shit seemed so far away. They'd transferred Raheem and Cashflow went to the hole. I was in the hole a week later. They did a random search and found a comb wit a razor on it that I usta cut my hair wit. They swore it was a weapon and they gave me thirty days in the hole for that shit. Our little group had pretty much came to an end. When I got out the hole two days later they transferred me to Fairbault.

CHAPTER 12

By now I was like "It's all time, wherever they send me to." It was no recording done at this facility and it wasn't no BET so I was shut down in that aspect. But I could still write and at that point I started writin only hooks. A section of the music business book put great emphasis on how important the hook of the song was, so I guess you can say this was the birth of my song writin career. That's all I did write hooks and re-read that music business book. I'd got a janitor job in the cottage so besides chow and the gym I never really left the cottage. I'd got a year's subscription to Source and Murdadog so I stayed informed through the homeys bout what was goin on in the hip hop world. When I could I'd catch Yo MTV Raps and that was like the highlight of the week. Someone had told me my homey Lew was down there but I hadn't seen him, then one day I was in the chow hall and someone yells.

"Yo Fleetwood what up blood!"

It was Lew, the homey had got swolled all up and was happy to see a nigga. After chow we smoked some weed and walked the yard then we started talkin bout music.

"Yo Fleet you ever heard of Master P?"

"Who" I said wit a curious look.

"Master P. 'I'm bout it bout it.' It's this nigga from New Orleans."

"I think I remember readin bout him in the Source but I haven't heard his music yet."

"Man you need to hear this shit. This nigga is country, west coast and has taken over the rap game."

"Why you say that?"

"Shit that nigga got a mob on his label and they all dope az fuck."

That night Lew let me borrow his CD player and the CD "Ice Cream Man." I was blowed away. This cat here was the truest shit I'd heard since Geto Boys. I must have listened to that CD 1,000 times. I couldn't believe this cat was right in Richmond, California takin the rap game over. When I left Cali it only was Too $hort in the Bay holdin down Oakland and then E-40 came out and I remember Frisco Kid, Coughnut and a cat from O.C. projects name O.C.O who had a song wit 4Tay called "Hubbles." But this Master P situation was all new. I'd been readin bout him though, along wit J.T the Bigga Figga, RBL Posse, Herm Lewis, Rappin 4Tay and San Quinn.

It was no secret Tupac had lit a fire in the bay. Pac was the nigga who held the bay down nationwide. He expressed our struggle so clearly. Wit all this jumpin off on my home turf I couldn't wait to get out and put my thang down in Minnesota and take my homeys and our music back to Cali. I dug real deep into the music book and read it over like 3 times. I had it down but I knew hands on experienced was a priceless lesson. No matter how much I read I knew I had to get out there in the mix to really understand how to get money in this music game. From what I understood L.P. and TLO had some cats listenin to our music in Florida who was feelin us so I was expectin to call the crib any day and hear that they had signed us. Little did I know things were goin in a completely different direction. I hadn't called home in maybe like two or three weeks.

"Hello J Dog what's up my nigga?"

"Wood what it is my nigga you get my letter?"

"N'all the mail been runnin slow I think they fuckin wit a nigga's mail. What's goin on"

"Man that stupid azz TLO got wrapped up wit some coke and a

pistol. He in the county right now lookin at four years."

"You bullshittin."

"Now you know I wouldn't bullshit bout nothin like that."

"How long ago this shit happen?"

"Shit it just happened last week. I wrote you the next day the letter should have been there."

"Damn I guess this mean everything gonna go on hold again until he get out."

"N'all wood we already discuss it. Me and TLO, we decided it's on us – me and you wood – we got to hold this shit down fo the crew till he come home."

'Well that's what we gonna do then, hold this shit down."

"My nigga call me tomorrow, I'm bout to bounce."

"J dog whatever you do, be careful you gotta stay free."

"Fo sho'."

Shit fucked me up. It was November of '96 and I had less than a year to come home and this shit jumps off. One day I received a letter from TLO tellin me he was on his way to that same fucked up boot camp and I couldn't stop laughin. I wrote him back and told him all the shit I went through up at that joint and how I had fucked up when I came home. After bout a month of him being at the camp he wrote me the same letter I wrote to my little sista, askin fo help wit these hillbilly crazy folks. Years later we would laugh bout this shit.

It was now the summer of '97 and I couldn't believe I was within months of goin home. One day we was hoopin and I got into it wit this nigga who went for bad. He had a gang of time to do and knew I was gettin short, so the nigga tried me. When we got back to the cottage he walked up on me and we got to chuckin but the homeys broke it up and luckily no guards seen us. Then I went to my room to change clothes and walked to the shower.

I wasn't sweatin that nigga but I knew I wasn't suppose to be walkin in no shower shoes, let alone goin to the shower alone after a confrontation. Even without a confrontation that was outta law because by doin that if I got into something and my folks assisted me I put my time and theirs in jeopardy and that wasn't good. This still was prison, an environment occupied by muthafuckas who really didn't give a fuck on the average. But I was just hot headed and was on some fuck that nigga shit. Anyways, I walked through the cottage to the shower in shower shoes wit a towel on, right past the nigga and he noticed I'm alone. I got in the shower and the next thing I know I heard this nigga'z voice.

"What's up Fleetwood? You gone come outta there or we gonna have to come in there to get you?"

I was in the shower butt azz naked wit no weapon tryin to pry the soap dish holder off the wall. I didn't know if these niggaz had knives or what, but whatever was gonna go down, it was gonna go down right then. Then I heard someone kick in the door.

"I don't know what the fuck y'all niggaz think y'all doin but that's a gangsta in there. Ya'll ain't bout to fuck wit folks in the shower." It was my kin folks.

"Nigga you wanna get whooped on some more? Wait till he get out the shower and get dressed."

I'mma always love my folks for that till ain't no breath left in me. If it wasn't for them I probably wouldn't be able to write this. The homeys was mad at a nigga for awhile though for puttin them in a fucked up position but eventually thangs were cool. That night I laid on my bed and decided I was gonna go hard at this music shit and not let nothin jeopardize my success ever again. I started writin crazy hooks and daily went over my plan of what I was gonna do when I got out. It was September 1997, one month from me goin home. I couldn't believe the shit. One afternoon niggaz came to my room.

"Fleet your boy got shot last night. It's all on the news."

"Who? What y'all talkin bout" I said.

"Tupac. They shot him up in Vegas after the Tyson fight."

My heart felt like it stopped and I got a funny feelin in my stomach. I was in a daze. This was my musical idol, but I was like "he gonna pull through," he'll be alright. For the next seven days I was watchin the news and just waitin to hear that he was gonna be alright. Then

I think after the fifth day they was like he lost consciousness. Two days later I heard the news. Tupac was dead.

For anybody in Northern California Tupac was like our brother, our homey. He rode for us. He described what we had been through and what we was goin through unlike anyone ever before and probably anyone ever after him. For the next three days I pretty much just moped around. Then finally one of my O.G's said "youngsta you gotta snap outta that shit you on, or you bout to be right back in here when you get out."

"What you mean" I asked.

"You got to continue to work on your plan to stay outta prison."

I laid on my bed and meditated for bout an hour or two and came to the conclusion that I had to get out, stay out and keep that fire lit that Tupac had sparked in the rap community, I wasn't bout to let nobody or nothin stop me.

CHAPTER 13

My out date finally came and it felt like my first birthday party. My homey Jabo was gonna come and get me but it was a mix up wit an old warrant so I had to go downtown to Minneapolis county for bout 9 hours, finally they called my name and I got my shit and I was walkin to the exit door. When that door clicked and opened to the streets it was like things went in slow motion for a minute.

I had a few dollars so I jumped in a cab headed for the Southside. L.P. had his own crib now and was doin his thang, plus he had a square job at a non profit. So I knocked on the door and everybody was happy to see a nigga.

I called me a breezy. "May I speak to Yolanda?"

"This her."

"What's up baby."

"Hey you out?"

"Yeah."

"What's the address?"

Thirty minutes later in walks Ms. Yolanda, thicker than frozen peanut butter. I met her while I was down and she'd stuck by me for 3 and a half years. The anticipation of our bodies touchin was amazin and when we hugged I could feel the heat between us. It wasn't twenty minutes after that we both were undressed and I was tryin hard to alter her spinal cord. After bout an hour of that shit, feelin like I had fought Tyson, a nigga passed out. I woke up and breezy was gone, but she had stuffed a nigga pocket wit a few hundred wit lipstick on em. The next day we had a meeting in Jason's livin room wit the whole crew: TLO was home, Major Damage, Jabo, L.P and Brickhead.

I led the meeting. "Look, this is what I feel we should do: Drop a compilation and create a buzz. Whoever is shinin at the time, we release their solo project."

"How we gonna fund all this wood? The last time you said that you ended up in prison" Jason asked.

"Well shit if y'all niggaz wanna pitch in cool but I'mma put this on my shoulders."

"Wood we can't let you do this by yourself we got you my nigga."

"Cool lets go in make some beats first, come back write hooks to them and then come back write rhymes and go back and drop the songs."

"Shit that sound good to me."

"So let me ask y'all this? How y'all feel bout the name "Probable Cause" I asked, not knowin how they would react.

We all agreed the name was hot and that the next thang was to get some hot tracks. Jabo had met this little young gangsta name Looney G who had just got out. We all met up one day and from the first line of his rhyme I knew he was dope, super dope. He had that new sound, that bounce flava. So we all started kickin it hard everyday and I realized it was gonna boil down to what it had before: money.

I wasn't bout to sign no neighborhood deal wit some balla and be his ho. I knew what I had to do, something I promised myself I wasn't gonna do again: hit the block. Here I was three weeks outta prison and on my way to see my man.

After the first sale it was like I had never left. I got my sac fat enough so I could afford runners and within a month I had my own apartment and a fat ride and fat pockets. One night we was vibin and I wrote this hook to this song called "They on Something" we went to the studio and recorded it the next day and we killed that shit. I knew leavin out the studio that we had a hit record, all we needed was the money to push it.

In a few days it was on the radio and that's when the buzz got crazy. I couldn't walk down the street without muthafuckas askin me to produce them. L.P. had this female that he was kickin it wit and she had two nephews that wanted to rap bad and wanted to meet me. So I got together wit them and one of them, "Gunny Gunny" really stood out. I told him I wanted him on my team. He had the look, the voice, and delivery but the only thang that scared me was that I knew he was gang bangin hard.

At the time I was also workin wit this young lady named Missy who usta be in the hood always swearing she could rap. I gave her the name "Fancy" and wrote her a song. After like 3 hours she had it down and I decided then that she was gonna be my Little Kim.

We were all together everyday, hustlin, gettin high and goin to the studio. We had almost fifteen songs recorded and I figured a few more and we'd be ready. We was already gettin radio play on the single " They on Something" so I arranged a photo shoot wit everybody and that day is when I realized that it was gonna be a problem.

L.P was a grown man now and no longer under my wing. I guess he felt like I was puttin too much energy into Looney G and Fancy. Plus, while I was down he'd flipped from Gangsta Disciple to Mickey Cobra and the Cobras at the time was doin damage in the streets. That was my homey and I still had love for him regardless, but Brickhead was also a Cobra, one wit rank, so we had like three Disciplines and two Cobras in our crew.

Eventually the drama in the streets separated us. L.P and me fell out, Brickhead was doin his thang and Major and Jabo went solo. So here I was left wit this album and basically Looney G and Fancy. My homeboy Robdog had got out and he was like:

"Fleet, what you need to do is take your shit back to California to your own turf."

"Rob I wanna go back home right. My niggaz out there ballin fo real feel me?"

"I feel ya my nigga but you keep hangin around here you might not make it back."

"Why you say that?"

"Cause these niggaz hatin on you cause they see in you what they always wanted to see in themselves."

"That ain't my fault though."

"I know it ain't but to get what you got comin you got to go back around niggaz of your caliber"

"Rob you right my nigga, you right. I'm up cuz'n."

At the time I was fuckin wit this cat from Chicago named Big Nasty signed to Island Def Jam and was real close wit Da Brat. He was like – "Floyd y'all shit dope my nigga. Let me lock this situation down wit Def Jam and I'mma bring y'all in."

"Cool folks, what you want me to do until then?"

"Shit, keep doin what you doin – creatin a buzz makin that hot shit because that's gonna make the whole process easier, you feel me?"

So for the next three weeks I grinded hard, stackin paper for the trip. Fancy was really by my side. On the block and everywhere I went Fancy was there. People just knew we was fuckin but that wasn't the case. Fancy was beautiful but she was only 16 and I knew keepin it brotha and sista wit her was for the best all around. Fancy's brotha had just got caught up on some drug charges and her moms was havin problems, so I was there for her and she recognized the real love and appreciated it. She was like:

"Floyd you ain't leavin me nigga."

"What you talkin bout?"

"You ain't goin nowhere without me."

"Is that right?"

"Yeah that's right, you stuck wit me."

"That might not be a bad thang though, you never know."

"Yeah you never know."

"Girl you something else."

"Whatever. I am gonna be right beside you and I ain't gonna let no one hurt you cause I know you ain't gonna let no one hurt me."

"You right bout that Fancy. You right bout that."

So one night I came to her and was like "you ready to go to Cali?" She thought I was bullshittin. Gunny had went back to Kansas City for a few weeks and Looney G had got locked up. So it was just me and Fancy. We had released the "Probable Cause" album, and it was doin good even though it was some inner group hatin jumpin off. In like three weeks though we had sold 2,000 cassettes locally. My homeboy "Smoke One", Q Bear and Jr. Maddox was showin us plenty of love at the local radio station.

"Grandma" – I usta call her that because she moved so slow – "Get your clothes packed, we bout to go to Cali tonite." She was excited as hell and ran up and hugged me. Damn near choked me to death.

"Fleetwood fo real? Fo real Fleetwood?"

"Yeah fo real. Get your clothes packed."

'What time we leavin?"

"The train leaves at 2 AM so be ready at midnite."

"Yeah I'll be ready you just better not be playin wit me."

"Girl just be ready when I call."

I really didn't tell no one I was bout to leave that night but that evening around 3PM, I got all my paper off the street and got the tickets at the train station. It was so much jealousy jumpin off and niggaz was gettin killed every other day. Muthafuckas felt like I thought I was Master P. so I was the target of a lot of the hate. I just couldn't breathe in the streets no more so it was time to go.

CHAPTER 14

When I came to get Fancy it was one of the happiest days of my life. The smile on this young lady's face and the love she had for me was incredible.

"Fleet we ain't comin home until we get on."

"Yeah I hear ya."

"I'm serious, till we get on."

"Don't even trip grandma, this is what you call destiny."

"What ever you call it we ain't comin without no connections."

It was so much bullshit jumpin off at the time I had really forgot that I was in the mist of pursuin my dream. I knew our music was hot and I knew they would feel it. It was just a matter of gettin it to the world. As the train pulled out of the St. Paul station I took a deep breathe and just stared out the window. It felt good to be goin back to Cali, before I knew it I was in a deep sleep on my way home.

After like ten hours passed by Fancy woke me up she was so excited it got me hyped. We walked through the train, got something to eat and talked.

"Fleetwood what's wrong?"

"You know I tried to really help them niggaz grandma, I never was out to fuck nobody."

"That's why them niggaz turned on you. Because they didn't know how to appreciate what you was doin for them."

"I think a lotta that shit had to do wit all that gang shit."

"It was partially that and also that them niggaz was jealous."

"Why you say that?"

"Because I usta hear them speak when you would leave the room. Niggaz was jealous of you Fleet."

"I don't even wanna know what was said but I do wanna know why you never came forward and told me what you tellin me now."

"Well because I was an outsider lookin in and I could also tell you had a lotta love for them and it probably would have been hard for you to believe."

"You right bout that Fancy. You definitely right."

"Well now the smoke is clear and you can see clearly now that the rain is gone. The only thang waitin on us is the California sunshine."

It was a beautiful thang to have someone believe in you so much that they would come across country not knowin what was awaitin them, finally after two and a half days on the train we were in the bay area. We got off the train and found our way to the BART. My grandparents stayed in the hills of Oakland and my little sisters stayed across the bridge in San Francisco. They lived in a hood called Fillmoe. This was the headquarters for JT the Bigga Figga's Get Low Records operation, so my little sistas house definitely would be the first stop. I was born in Kaiser Hospital on Geary Street and stayed in the Fillmoe until mom and pop divorced.

Fillmoe was always like my hood in San Francisco even though I didn't actually grew up there, I had family ties and was always in the hood. I knew quite a few O.G.'s and hustlas in Fillmoe like Darryl Luckett, Creature Man and Rolls Royce, just to name a few. I didn't know this younger generation of emcee's but they were my little sista's folks and that was all I needed. Me and Fancy got off the BART in downtown Frisco in the Tenderloin, a.k.a. the L's.

Her reaction was the same as any person who sees downtown San Francisco for the first time. She couldn't believe her eyes. As we got on the bus and headed up the street to Fillmoe I'll neva forget, Fancy turned and looked at me and said

"Now I see why you can hustle the way you can and why you so wild and crazy."

"Why you say that?"

"That place look like a jungle Fleet."

"I wouldn't say all that, it's just the L's grandma. It's just the L's"

"Shit I ain't never seen nothin like that in my life. Even that movie New Jack City can't even fuck wit that."

I just started laughin. It was something I'd heard quite a few times before. We go to the Banneker homes where my family was. I had hollered at my sista bout a month before so she was expectin me I thought. It never really clicked in my mind the repercussions of travelin wit an under age female. I knew she hadn't ran away and her moms had okayed it so I figured it was cool. But as soon as I walked into my little sistas house wit Fancy they all had a look like "nigga is you crazy what is you doin wit this young azz girl?" My step mom took me in the back and grilled me bout how much trouble I could get into by travelin wit a minor.

"Robert how old is that girl?"

"She 16."

"Boy have you lost your damn mind?"

"What you talkin bout Sherry? Her moms know she wit me and she ain't no runaway or nothin like that."

"But still though you can't be travelin across the state lines wit a minor without written permission and the parents consent."

"I do have her consent."

"Do you have it on paper?"

"No ma'am."

"That's what I'm talkin bout. The police would put you under the jail thinkin you out here pimpin this young girl."

"Pimpin her? That's my rap protégé."

"I know what she is and you know, but what you gotta understand is how it looks."

"I understand."

"Do you really?"

'Yes ma'am."

"What's that girl's mother phone number?"

Every chance they got they grilled Fancy bout what was I to her. She told 'em Fleetwood is like my brother which was true. To this day they still think I was on something bogus wit Fancy. Anyway Fancy and my youngest sista Asia were close in age so she chilled wit them while I went down to the T.L. I wanted to run into some of my old homeys and by the time I got back Fancy was all excited like it was her birthday or something.

"Fleet! Fleet! Guess what nigga" she said smilin and dancing around like she had to pee.

"Damn what's wrong wit you grandma" I said wit a curious look.

"Guess what?"

"What grandma?"

"I met this nigga that like me, his name J.T. the Bigga Figga. I told him I rap and bout you and he want to hear my song. I told him you produced it."

This was the nigga I came to meet! See, it was something real special bout Fancy. The same guy who I had just read bout in Vibe Magazine sittin in my room in prison less than a year earlier. The article was all bout how this young black brotha was carvin his way into the music industry by being black-owned and independent, always stressin the importance of ownin your own masters. I knew wit me and her in the right environment we was gonna make connections, but I never expected it to happen so fast. Now here I was wit Fancy at my little sista house waitin on JT the Bigga Figga to come hear our song.

The door bell rang and in walked this tall lanky dude and his homey. Fancy kicked in. One thing I never had to worry bout wit Fancy was her being confident.

"J.T. what you bout to hear gonna fuck you up. It's some of that shit."

"Is that right?"

"Hell yeah Fleetwood made the beat and wrote the hook, we wrote the rhyme together"

"What's up homey? Fleetwood" I said extending my hand.

"JT. This the commissioner Devo One of the Gamblaz" he said lookin at his homey. "So where this dope azz song I'm suppose to be hearing?"

"Fleet you ready?"

"Fo sho'."

I push play on the box and as soon as the beat dropped Fancy came in wit the hook. I looked and I knew we had 'em.

"That shit hot family. I got a soundtrack comin out for my movie, "Beware of Those." You wanna put that song on the sound track?"

"Hell yeah my nigga" I said, maybe a little too excited.

"Well look, I got a few moves to make but I'll be back and I want y'all to come to my studio."

"Cool."

"Here's the number, hit me in two hours."

As he was leavin Fancy was like "let me ride wit you around till you come back." I knew what she was doin: makin sure we wasn't bout to lose contact wit him. JT looked at me and we went outside.

"Look cuz'n that's my soulja, don't let nothin happen to her. Please brotha, fancy like my little sista."

"So that ain't your work?"

'N'all fig, that's family homey."

He assured me that she was in good hands and they'd be back in a few hours. I was like cool, I knew I had laced Fancy enough in Minnesota to handle herself so I wasn't worried shit. I went back to the L's and waited for their call. I ran into my nigga Psycho D.

I walked up. "Psyche, look there go black azz Fleetwood, pimpin azz" said Chill, one of the homeys.

"What's up Psych?" We called him that because this nigga was O Dog in livin color, way before Menace 2 Society. No sense of remorse for nothin but if you knew him he was a real good dude. He just was a reflection of what the streets will turn you into.

"Fleetwood where the fuck you been?"

"Shit my nigga I been in Minnesota and back down south. You know me Psych. I'm a globe trotter"

"My nigga ya boy need you back down here wit him, real talk. You got to be one of the craziest, realest niggaz I know."

"Psych you know I love ya boy but this ain't for me no more family."

"What you talkin bout? You help build this shit Fleetwood."

"My nigga I had to change my life or these white folks was gonna change it for me. That's what I would advise you to do, feel me?"

"I feel ya my nigga. Maybe one day. Maybe one day."

"What's been happenin down here though?"

"Same shit: dope fiends gone wild. Punk azz jump out boys chasin niggaz, whoopin them when they catch them and these bogus azz niggaz tryin to smash through our hood. That's why I need you back down here wit me Fleet."

"Psych I fucks wit that rap shit now. I'm bout to go meet JT the Bigga Figga in Fillmoe right now."

"Tell that nigga Psych said what up."

"Look I want you to come back to Minnesota. Give this shit a break."

"I'm wit that shit my nigga, I'm wit that shit. But you know this ours right here Fleet. We built this shit."

"Yeah but it's a new day. It's a new day Psych."

After a while I think he realized how serious I was bout the rap game and he told me to put my same hustle down and wished me the best. I walked around a little while longer through the woo block (brown weed only), saw a few more homeys then my pager went off. It was Fancy.

"Fleet come on, where you at? We ready to go to the studio."

I made my way back up to Fillmoe and that night we went to the studio and it was all love. This nigga JT was showin me the kinda love you don't usually get in the music industry, that's why I'll always have love for that dude. Me and JT made a beat that night that was super hot. He told me he was gonna do everything he could to help us get on.

He said "Look wood this what you do: go back to Minnesota, get your dats and I'mma put you on."

"Figgaro it might take a week or two, but I'll be back trust me."

"Cool my nigga I'll be waitin on ya."

Later on that night as we were leavin the studio this group "Fully Loaded" came in. Within thirty minutes we had finished up at JT's and we were now at Fully Loaded Studio, the home of Big Rich. It was all love and we vibed all night makin tracks and rhymin. They all were Fancy's age or a year older so they really bonded. During the next two days I took Fancy all around the bay. Between me and JT showin her around she was sprung. I saw it in her eyes she was in love wit California.

CHAPTER 15

We caught the train back to Minnesota and all I could think of was gettin back to Cali. Not like "fuck Minnesota", but I just finally had an inside plug in the music game and I was gonna do anything I could to get back to get on so I could get my homeys on. When we finally got back to Minnesota everybody was mad cause I had took Fancy wit me, especially Gunny. His dream was to go to Cali so he made me promise that I'd take him wit me the next time I went. A few days passed and I was gettin my chips up so I could return to Cali. I made sure I stayed in touch wit JT.

"Yeah?"

'Figgaro this Fleetwood."

"What up wood?"

"Just grindin. Gettin, my chippers up so I can come back up there."

"How little fancy doin?"

"She cool but I had to shut her down for minute cause she wasn't goin to school."

"Yeah you did the right thang."

"I got bout 20 new songs, bout another week and I should be ready."

"Cool my nigga, just give me a call."

"One love."

"One love."

After a week passed I was almost ready and right at that time I started havin problems wit Fancy goin to school – all she wanted to do was hustle and flow. But we had an agreement from the jump: no school, no studio. So we fell out and she was mad but I felt it was for the best. A few days passed and one night I was on the block and a hype came through wit a dope fiend rental. I was in the pen wit him so he trusted me. I gave him 6 slugs.

"Check this out cuz'n I'll bring it back at 6AM."

"Fleetwood man don't let nothin happen to my car."

"Bossman I gotcha."

"Okay see you in the mornin."

As soon as I dropped the hype off at his house I called Gunny.

"Hello?"

"Gunleno!"

"What up Wood?"

"You wanna go to Cali?"

"Hell yeah folks when?"

"Right now. Get your clothes packed."

"Wood don't be bullshittin now."

"Look I ain't bullshittin. Be ready in 2 hours."

"Wood can the homey Skeet come?"

"He got some gas money?"

"That little nigga got astronaut paper!"

"Yeah bring him then. Tell that nigga leave them pistols on the North Side. We ain't ridin like that."

I had made up in my mind. Fuck waitin and riskin gettin caught up on the block, I was 'bout to drive back to Cali. See, I had finally found something in life that I was good at besides sports. Hip hop was for all the niggaz in the hood who didn't get that Michael Jordan dream; who never was gonna make it to the NFL or NBA. This was their chance at stardom, it gave them shine in the hood and made them a star, feel me? It gave them a sense of worth.

This was why so many of the homeys would hustle on the block all day and night just for studio time. Being a rapper gave them hope,

like "one day I can get outta this ghetto if I grind hard enough."
Sometimes in life you gotta go for what you believe in and I believed
in the art of hip hop. I knew it had a spot for me and I knew I could
make it in the game. Now that I had a solid major plug I wasn't gonna
let this pass me by. I was on some shit like "they gonna have to catch
me" and I'd be on the side of the road in some hick town or I'd be
back in Cali in the studio wit JT. I wasn't gonna be sittin somewhere
years from that moment thinkin "what if?" Feel me? So it was time
to smash and that's what I did. In life what don't kill you will make
you stronger and I knew if I made it the experience would make me
stronger. That's how much I loved hip hop – enough to risk it all. It
was tryin to kill me cause I loved it so, feel me?

I figured by the time mornin came we'd be half way to the Fillmoe.
This was a chance I was gonna have to take. I didn't tell Gunny I was
in a dope fiend rental and he didn't even ask. He just wanted to know
if the homey Skeet could ride wit us. Shit an hour later we was headed
out of Minnesota on the highway. Right when we hit Wisconsin State
line the Highway Patrol pulled us over. I knew the car couldn't be
reported stolen that fast but what I was worried bout was my L's. I
wasn't sure if they were suspended or not.

"May I see your license and registration please?"

"No problem officer. If you don't mind could you please tell me
what I did wrong?"

"Well you were goin kinda slow and swervin. I just wanted to make
sure y'all were alright."

"Yeah we cool. It's just hard to see wit all this snow comin down
like it is."

"I understand completely. Just hold on and I'll be right back."

Sittin there on the side of the highway all I could visualize was
sittin back in one of those prisons, thinkin how I had fucked off my
golden opportunity. Then the officer knocked on the window and
handed me my license.

"Drive safe gentlemen, it's reported that the snow is gonna get
even worse and come down harder."

"Thank you very much officer. We'll be careful, have a good night."
'You to" he said walkin away.

I exhaled as I rolled up the window and smashed off. Gunny and Skeet didn't really say shit as I turned up the music. It was our destiny to get to California. Ten hours later we was sittin in Omaha, Nebraska at a McDonald's and I told them bout the car.

"Say Gunny man, this car is a steamer."

'What? Folks you know you bogus fo havin us in a stolen car."

"Man it might not even be reported yet."

"Fuck that you should have told us from the jump. Skeet, man this nigga got us in a steamer goin cross country."

"Shit, fuck it. I ain't drivin. That's on him."

"Yeah Gunny if it go down I'll tell the law y'all didn't know."

"Let's go my nigga."

Twenty minutes later we back on the highway. I put the cruise control on and kept smashin. A day later we in Nevada, one state from California and by now I knew the car had been reported stolen, but I also knew what I had to do. I had to get back to the Fillmoe fast. As we passed through Sacramento on the highway I couldn't believe I was less than an hour from the bay. The only thing goin through my mind was get this car to the Fillmoe and get wit JT.

That was the moment I realized I was addicted to hip hop the rap game: the studio, the rhymes, the beats. Hip hop gave me a chance to express myself. I'd finally found something I had a passion fo.

CHAPTER 16

So here was me, Skeet, and Gunny finally in Oakland, headed across the Bay Bridge on our way to San Francisco. We was so hyped I think we all forgot the car was even stolen. As I came on the exit at 6th St. downtown San Francisco I thought to myself what better way to introduce my homeys to California than to take them through the T.L. On the real I felt like I couldn't get caught and we came through the T.L doin a good hundred! This was the hottest hood in the city and I was drivin a stolen car but you'd never have knew it from the way I was drivin. I pulled over in the heart of it on Eddy and Jones St. We jumped out. I looked over at Gunny and Skeet and their face had the same expression as everyone else who has ever seen the TL for the first time, like "what the fuck?" It was niggaz shootin dope in broad day light on the sidewalk, niggaz smokin dope, ho's walkin around, drag queens everywhere and the punk azz cops hittin the corna every 5 minutes. This was a world of it's own that most people have never thought bout visitin . We jumped out and I introduced them to some O.Gs, then we blowed some Cali weed and got back in the car and bounced up the street to Fillmoe.

I stopped by my little sista Attica's house and parked the steamer. She opened the door wit her blue uniform and boots on ready to go to work. She was a firewoman in San Francisco and I was very proud of her. She stood their wit a look on her face like nigga what the hell is goin on?

"Robert how you get back up here?"

"I drove."

"What you mean you drove you just told me last week on the phone you didn't have a car?"

"Well I gave this dude something to use his car."

"And he let you drive it all the way to California?"

'No, not exactly."

"So what you sayin is you drove a stolen car out here?"

"It ain't reported stolen yet" I said smilin.

"Nigga you is crazy fo real! Where the damn car at wit your stupid azz? Y'all two gonna end up in prison right along wit him."

"Tica I'm tryin to get on, I needed to come back. That's the only option I had."

"No that's the option your dumb azz chose."

"Man can you loan me some money please?"

"Boy you need some help. And how you just gonna pop up at my house unannounced" she said lookin at me, not givin a fuck how Gunny and them took it.

"Man you told me I could come anytime I wanted to last week. You forgot?"

"Yeah but you still should've call me first. What if I would have been outta town."

"I would have figured something else out."

"Here boy, now get your hot azz somewhere." She let us put our bags there and gave me some loot before I bounced.

"And whatever you do don't get back in that car."

I called JT and he couldn't believe I was back that fast.

"Fig this Fleetwood."

"What up blood?"

"Figgaro I'm in Fillmoe."

"You in the Mo?"

"Hell yeah I told I was comin back."

"You bring the dats wit you?"

"Fo sho'."

"Meet me at the lab in thirty minutes."

"Down."

"Down."

The studio was up the street so we walked through the hood. The young homeys thought I was from Minnesota and they was feelin the fact that we had came all the way out there to their hood. Man, it was all love.

We got to the studio and exchanged pounds and it was like five or six dudes in the lab listenin to a beat and writin. Seff the Gaffla – this nigga here reminded me of Tupac, then San Quinn – he was laid back like on some smooth shit just peepin us, then it was Devo – he was part of the Gamblaz, a group signed to JT's Get Low Records. It was also this cat hella quiet in the corna. All he kept sayin was play the beat again. This was Messy Marv.

San Quinn had to go handle something but the rest of them stayed and finished writin. JT pulled up the beat we had made and as soon as it came on them niggaz was like "damn" and started writin again. I had been wrote my verse and I was ready. To be honest I had never been in a room writin wit so many people and I think it would've been hella hard for me to concentrate, but this was how they did it. Everybody was ready and Messy came on first. I was blown away by the cleverness of his rhymes. As the song grew wit everyone's verse it kept gettin stronger and stronger and their rhymes was super hot. Each person had a unique style that was phenomenal. JT and Gunny capped it off. I ended it and Gunny did the outro. We decided to call the song "From the Filthy to the Shady" meanin from Fillmoe to Minnesota. We had made a classic and we all knew it. Nigga it was a wrap, we had created an underground smash that fast.

I couldn't believe these dope azz niggaz had got down on the song for free. Not once did they ask me for anything but to let Minnesota know its love in Fillmoe. Later that night we hung out for awhile then me and Skeet and Gunny went and crashed at my little sista's house.

The next day we got back up wit JT and rode around to do some street team shit. The whole time I was in his ear 'bout the game and the more we talked the more I realized it was time to move permanently back to Cali. Basically he explained to me that Minnesota was good for Prince. They did their thing up there but for someone who really wanted to be in the rap game and be a CEO and own a independent label, the bay. my home, was the heartland. This was were I needed to be and I couldn't agree more. This was where I needed to be.

We kicked it a few more days and then I told Gunny and Skeet we were gonna bounce the next day. Them niggaz looked at me.

"Nigga you crazier than a road lizard. We ain't bout to ride back in that hot azz car cross country" Gunny said lookin at me serious.

"Yeah Wood I'm catchin me a plane outta here tomorrow I can't fuck wit that hot azz car" said Skeet.

"Shit" said Gunny. "I'mma hop on the Greyhound. It's gonna take three days but fuck it. It'll give me time to think."

"I understand my nigga. I got no other choice though. I got to ride this one on out."

"Your azz just crazy that's all" said Attica, eavesdroppin from the side line.

"What you talkin bout?" I said surprised.

"You be on some dumb shit to be so damn smart. I don't understand you sometimes."

My little sista was mad at me cause I was on some wild "hip hop or die" shit. But I knew I had to get back to Minnesota and get back to Cali. I only had one way – the streamer – so that's how I was goin. I had smashed out here so I was gonna smash back, ride or die time again, feel me? "All in a day of a hip hop life" that's how I looked at it, never second guessin myself at all. My money was hella funny so I called JT.

"Fig, what up homey?"

"Wood what's the bizn?"

"Man I'm bout to pull out get back to the 'Sota, get all my shit and move back to the bay."

"Where ya homeys at?"

"One caught the bus and other got a plane ticket but I gotta drive this steamer back."

"How your pockets lookin?"

"My nigga I'm leakin bad."

"Look, where you at?"

"I'm on Webster and Grove at Attica's house."

"Stay right there. I'll be there in a few minutes."

As I paced back and forth on the sidewalk waitin on him I was comin up wit Plan B just in case he didn't come through. Because honestly he really didn't owe me nothin. He had been real wit me the whole time, something that was rare in the game so I kinda knew he was gonna come through for me. The nigga was real, I knew that.

"Shitted, it wasn't three minutes JT pulled up, jumped out and walked over to me.

"What up cuz'n" he said then extended his hand gave me a pound wit a wad of money in his hand.

"Here you go. Be careful and keep your phone on my nigga."

"Fo sho'. Boy I love you fo this Fig."

"Don't even trip my nigga don't even trip."

Me and JT bonded real quick. There was a certain respect and even though he was major he never fronted on me. Before I got on the highway I figured it would be a good idea to call back to Minnesota to see if the car had been reported stolen. It had been, but I didn't give a fuck. I had to get back to get my shit so I hit the highway.

I'll neva forget ridin through those mountains in Utah, fish tailin in the snow and not knowin if I was gonna make it or not. As the hours passed and the big tractor trailer trucks zoomed passed me I was gettin closer and closer. Finally I made it to Nebraska, to that same McDonald's we had stopped at on the way up there. I had just got off the phone wit JT. He was a real nigga. He called me like five or six times to check on me. That was some real shit. My money was gettin low but I knew I had enough to make it to Iowa. After that I was fucked. I called my homey Robdog.

"Dog this Fleetwood what up?"

"Woodstock where you at? You back yet?"

"Hell n'all. my nigga, I'm just comin into Iowa. I need some ends fo some gas to get back."

"Give me like 30 minutes and it'll be there."

"Cool, one love my nigga."

"One love."

I went to the local Western Union and the bread was there. I filled up the steamer and kept smashin until finally I was entering St. Paul, the next city was Minneapolis. My crazy azz smashed right through the hood and who did I see on the corner but Gunny. I'll never forget the look on his face. I took the car back to the head and when I rung his doorbell I really didn't know how he was gonna react. I was like "fuck it, at least he got his car back." The nigga came out and couldn't believe it was me when I gave him his keys.

"Man where you been?"

"Yo I had a emergency, feel me? But your car cool."

"Man, damn though Fleetwood. You been gone almost a month wit my car though."

"Look I'mma throw you something later on tonight for your inconvenience."

"Man it got to be right. My ol lady ready to kill me. She damn near left me behind this shit."

"Well this is a lesson. Don't be loanin your car out fo no dope my nigga."

"That's some fucked up shit to say."

"Look my nigga, I said I was gonna hit you wit something and I will" and I did later that night. But one thing I never anticipated was the hate that was still waitin on me.

CHAPTER 17

Everybody had got the word I was in Cali making moves. While we was in Cali I called my homey Smoke One at the radio station and me and JT the Bigga Figga did a hot interview, plus Gunny was everywhere in the city letting people know Fillmoe was the shit. So when I got Smoke One to play "From the filthy 2 the Shady" it was over. No matter where I went niggaz was hating on me like "this nigga think he Master P."

It already was hella funk in the streets with that gang shit and now niggaz I was down wit before had their O.G's in their ear like "that nigga using ya'll to get on." I couldn't believe the shit! I wasn't there two days and some nigga studio got hit. Somehow these niggaz pointed the finger right at me. One night I'm at First Avenue, the downtown nightclub where they filmed Purple Rain. I was peeping out "The Lost Boys" and I had just finished hollering at Stephon Marbury when some nigga came up on me – "What's up homey, your name Fleetwood."

"Yeah what's the bizn my nigga?"

"You that punk mutha fucka that broke in my studio nigga."

"Say what? What the fuck you talking bout?"

"Nigga you know what I'm talking bout."

"Nigga I fucks with hitters on the west coast, what the fuck I need you punk az studio for?"

That's when I noticed niggaz in the cut coming towards me. These niggaz was bout to do me! I grabbed an empty bottle off the table and was ready for whatever. Right then security came between us. I knew all the security so they was making sure I was good. Right after that all the niggaz in the cut disappeared but that one nigga kept shadowing me so I knew – Death was outside that club. These niggaz was plotting on my life.

"Dog this Wood I need some help cuz."

"What's up?"

"Man these niggaz came at me crazy. I'm up here at First Avenue Downtown."

"What they talking bout?"

"They think I broke in there punk ass studio, man I just got back in town!"

"Don't worry bout that shit I'm on my way, I got Chicken George with me."

"Cool. I'm in the back of the club call my phone when you get up in here."

Robdog and the homey was there in five minutes and we had enough heat to warm Alaska. Plus Robdog was a shot caller and he made a few calls and the shit was suppose to be dead. But still, as I walked outta that club I knew that if I stayed in the city I'd be dead or back in the pen in a month.

"Woodstock, fuck them ho azz niggaz" Robdog told me, "get back to Cali and solidify that connection with JT. Cause if you stay here you gonna end up back in the pen or dead fucking with these, niggaz feel me?"

That next day I'm on a Greyhound on my way back to Cali and the Fillmoe. All I could think of was "I'm in this rap shit till I die." I had called JT and told him I was on my way back.

"Wood just call me as soon as you get back I'll come and get you" JT said.

"Fo sho my nigga."

Finally I made it to the San Francisco Greyhound station. It was good to be away from all the bullshit and I thought now maybe I could breathe, I called JT and couldn't catch him so I called the studio.

"Studio" said the man's voice on the other end.

"Yo this Fleetwood JT there?"

"N'all Fleetwood, what up boy this Messy."

"Mess what up my nigga I'm back in the Sco. I'm at the bus station I need a ride"

"Man ain't nobody here."

I jumped in a cab and in fifteen minutes I was in Fillmoe. Damn, shit was going good so that night me and Messy kicked it with some breezy's in the studio. JT called and said he'd get up with me in the morning. Bout six o'clock the females left and I had some shit I had to take care of in Oakland. Messy left walking and the dude who house it was was still there with a few people. Later, I'm walking back up the street towards the studio and the homey Devo tells me – "Fleet the studio got hit."

"Got what?"

'Some niggaz ran up in there, JT been looking for you where you been?"

"Man I had to go handle something downtown."

"Well JT and Quinn up there, go holla at them." I couldn't believe this shit. I went straight to the lab. San Quinn and JT was sitting there. JT was calm but I could tell he was mad as fuck.

"My nigga where you been" said JT as I walked in.

"I had to go to the GA office to get settled in."

"What happened last night?"

"Bout 6 AM me and Messy left and it was still a gang of people here. The owner of the house was here so I thought it was cool Fig. I didn't know what these muthafuckas was plotting."

He knew I didn't have nothing to do with the shit but he was like "My nigga I pretty much done did everything I can do for you right now. I got to concentrate on getting Get Low Records back in order."

"I feel ya. I appreciate everything you've did homey."

"You gonna be straight?"

"Yeah I'll be alright."

I understood but I couldn't believe this shit! I'd just left some bull-shit in Minnesota bout a fucking studio then this shit happens, fuck-ing me up. I didn't know but one thing to do. I took all my shit to my grandmother's house in Oakland and went back to the T.L. I was back in survival mode.

It was 1999. El Nino was raining hard and I couldn't believe I was right back on these corners, the same corners I swore I'd never pitch on again, selling crack for a hotel room and food.

I did that stupid shit for about a month and luckily I didn't get snatched. I stayed in touch with Gunny and Robdog and my cousin down south They all had the same thing to say "fuck that block shit get back in the studio, that rap game is your calling." But I knew I needed money to get my operation off the ground. This shit was all about money and connections, and I had no money and my connect had told me "right now you got to get it yourself."

So one night I'm on the block and them jump out boys jumped out. I was dirty ass hell but they ran right pass me and snatched like five cats right off the block. I saw my life flash. I walked away from that shit and decided once again to try to walk away from the game. The next day I went out looking for a job.

For those who don't know San Francisco this is one of the most expensive places to live in the US. I needed money to get me a crib and I wasn't sure how much faith I could put in this square shit but I was willing to try. In a couple of days I got lucky and got into a Janitorial Union paying decent money but the only thing was I got off of work at 2 AM and the trains to Oakland stop running at 1AM. That meant I had no way to get to my grandmothers house in the hills. Since I wasn't hustling no more so I couldn't afford a hotel room every night so I had two choices: bump me a breezy with a crib or go to the shelter. I wasn't trying to get thrown out in the middle of the night fucking with one of them females in the hood so I went to the shelter. I could sleep and save my paper. It turned out to be a blessing in disguise.

After about three weeks I found out one of the security guards was a hot producer from Hunter's Point with a studio – the same cat I'd be speaking to every night when I came in. It took a few days but I finally caught up with him, his name was Mr. Laid, one of the coolest niggaz I ever met. I let him hear the song I did with JT and Messy, Seff and Devo and he knew I had talent.

"Look Fleet I'ma help ya my nigga cause I can see you trying hard bro."

"I really appreciate it homey you won't regret it I promise" I told him.

He helped me and didn't know me from Adam. That was some real shit. Laid, if I ever come up I got you. Trust that shit homie.

One night I came into the shelter and it was a message for me to call my grandmother. Right when I heard her voice I knew something was wrong.

"Robert" she said in a sad voice.

"Yes big mama what's wrong?"

"Robert" she said starting to cry this time.

"Big Mama what's wrong? Big mama what's wrong!" I was screaming now, I didn't know what to expect.

"Robert you father is dead."

"He's dead? What you mean?

"He had a car accident on the way home from work and he went into a seizure after the accident. He never regained consciousness."

"Oh my God Big mama lord have mercy."

"Robert we're going back to North Carolina in two days. We know you're working hard trying to get back on your feet baby. We'll go if you can send some flowers."

"Yes ma'am. When ya'll leaving?"

"Tomorrow baby."

"Make sure you call me before ya'll get on that plane. Big Mama?"

"Yes Robert?"

"I love you."

"I love you too baby."

The phone went dead and I just held the receiver for a minute in a daze. Even though we weren't hella tight dude still was my father. My dad was a country boy who got blinded by the big city lights. That's probably what made him and my moms split. Moms was spiritual inside and out, that's where I get mine from. I still remember every time I came to visit my dad would have a new caddy and we lived in these big azz cribs in the suburbs in Daly City South San Francisco. The older I got I realized pops was the dope man.

About two years prior I had got another call telling me that my pops had been ambushed by some niggaz in North Oakland. I remember him being in a coma after that and my grandmother having to pretty much re-raise him. After he regained his mobility and coordination Big Mama talked him into moving back down south and he did, but he had a seizure while driving, wrecked his car and died. Man that's some ill shit.

No matter what he did to feed the family that was my daddy and I loved him so pop please – REST IN PEACE.

CHAPTER 18

After bout two months I got my own apartment. One night I was hollering at Gunny.

"Fleet man, I'm bout to comeback to Fillmoe my nigga. It's crazy in the streets of Minnesota right now. I might not make it too much longer."

"I feel ya Gunleno, that's why I got the fuck from up out there."

"I saw Fancy."

"You did? Where?"

"Over North."

"Ay give her my number and tell her to call me."

Fancy called me and we squashed our little bullshit. We had too much love for each other and all she talked bout was comin back to Cali. They both stayed in touch wit JT but I hadn't seen or heard from him in almost a year. Anyway, I was formin a crew again. I plugged in wit Mr. Laid and I met two brothers from the West Point projects in Hunters Point I knew from doin some street team shit wit JT. They was dope and I told them I was gonna fuck wit them when I got right. The younger brotha's name was Larceny and the older laid back one was Hectic. Even though I wasn't on the block I still came through the T.L everyday I worked. One day I was talkin to my homeboy Mr. Exclusive.

"Fleet, listen man I founded her."

"Found who?"

"I found that girl that's gonna complete your circle."

"Is that right? How is that?"

"I ain't never heard no female like her before she dope fo real."

"So what's her name?"

"She dope fo real!"

"So what's her name?"

"She calls herself Midnite Blu."

"Midnite Blu huh? That's different, where she be at?"

"She be down here in the TL my nigga."

"Well set it up."

When I heard her rhyme I knew she was dope. She had a very deep voice that was comin out of a small frame body. She kinda looked like Tupac a little wit long hair. I usta always kid her bout that but her voice was so raw. Vocal tone is very important and what I always look for and she had a different tone compared to most women who grab the mic. It was deep and raspy but still smooth and she had like a off beat rhyme style, overlappin the beat. She was definitely the final piece to my puzzle. So within three days we was at Mr. Laid's studio recording our project. I decided to name the group "Minimum Wage." It wasn't like I had forgot bout Gunny and Fancy but I needed a crew that I could get out and perform wit.

Besides the janitorial job I was also doin a little temp work on the side and one day I met this cat from Long Beach who was down wit DJ Chilli Chill of the Lynch Mob. We were workin in a store doin overnight inventory.

"What's up homey my name Fleetwood."

"Mac Dub, you from San Francisco?"

"Yeah I'm from the whole bay really."

"I'm from Long Beach up here workin, doin this inventory and travelin wit this company."

"You say you from Long Beach, you know Snoop?"

'Yeah cuz I know him, but we got our own thang, me and Chilli

Chill" he told me he was from Curbside. This nigga was so dope, you know I brought him in the studio. By that time Fancy and Gunny came back out to Cali and it was all love. The family was back together again and everything was goin cool. They pretty much was at home so I didn't have to baby sit them this time. While they were there we kicked it wit JT. We all met up on Market St. downtown San Francisco at a record store. We walked in and seen JT in the back, negotiating as usual networkin, business conductin.

"What's up Fig?"

"How you doin brotha? Long time I ain't seen you Wood."

"Yeah man I just been workin, layin low, stayin out the way feel me?"

"I feel ya my nigga. Well get at me though you got the numbers."

'Fo sho' one love."

"One love."

It was the first time I had talked to him in a while. It was still all love but it wasn't no more free recording jumpin off, which I understood. Plus my bread was kinda funny and Mr. Laid was givin me a cool price. I told JT what I was doin and he was like just stay at it. Gunny and Fancy left and I kept grindin. One day my homeboy Mr. Exclusive told me – "Yo Wood I met this nigga on the BART, his name is Boots you ever heard of him?"

"Boots? N'all."

"He got a group called the Coup from Oakland."

"Oh yeah I heard of them what's up wit him?"

"Man you know they been tryin to pass that Prop 21 law bout juveniles and shit."

"Yeah I heard."

"Well he puttin out a compilation bout it, formin really a whole movement and he's lookin for someone from San Francisco to rep wit him. I told him bout you he said he was gonna call."

"Pimpin that's good lookin out" I said as I dapped him up and hugged him showin my gratitude.

"Yeah Fleet you know how we do it."

'Fo sho."

When dude called me at first I thought it was some muthafucka on some bullshit.

"What up?"

"Hello?"

"Yeah hello who this?"

"Say this Boots from The Coup."

"Who?"

"Boots from The Coup. I met your homeboy on the BART. He was tellin me bout you."

"Oh okay. What's up homey?"

"Listen I need that San Francisco perspective bout this law they tryin to pass and I was told you're a very powerful voice in the 'Sco."

"Yeah that's a true story and I'm definitely ready to rep fo ya."

"So what's the name of your group?"

"Minimum Wage homey."

"Minimum Wage? Damn that's hot. So you produce and rap huh?"

"All day everyday homey."

"Well put together something bout the cause and I'mma get back at you."

"No problem cuzn, no problem."

Meetin up wit this cat Boots was the beginning of me being involved in the revolution. My music was always conscious, political and street from the Dope Boyz music I had started wit. I was partially raised in the south so I saw and experienced racism a little different than people in the west but it was all the same bullshit and out here you could speak your mind more. This was the heart of fuck the government and police type shit. I always wanted to reach my people, be on some Ice Cube type shit, feel me? Now I had the chance to really be in the midst of the war, the fight for the liberation of my people and I couldn't wait to get started.

At the time they were tryin to pass a law in California – Proposition 21, that sent juveniles to prison at the age of fourteen, said police could arrest any group of four or more people dressed alike for felony loitering and gave them the authority to go back in your juvenile criminal record and use that against you. So you could have been on your job ten years and they check your Juvenile record and they could fire you.

I had already been goin to group homes speakin to the youth bout my life wit my homeboy Bizzy Ben and his Straight Forward club. But this was something totally different. After me and Boots hollered that night me and Midnite Blu wrote this song called "Prop 21." It was hot and Boots loved it.

For like the next two months we would go to different high schools on a flat bed truck, pull up right when school was lettin out at like 3 PM and just rock until the police came. In a way this was crazy. My whole life I been on the block hustlin and dodgin the police and now here I was waitin for the police to come it was like still fuck them. So I guess that's what gave me the rush, defyin the law. I really was feelin what we were doin. Eventually we went and recorded the song and performed on a TV show.

This is when I met Davey D, the famous hip hop journalist, at a function in Oakland. After meetin him that night we appeared on his radio show, he was fo real and showed me love. To this day that's the homey. Thangs were goin well, they had the song scheduled to be put on a compilation and during this time I met the homey T-Kash who host's a radio show in Berkley on KPFA. There was also this dude name J.R., who is now a top journalist in the bay, who works real close wit Fred Hampton Jr. in the POCC. It was a spot Boots took me to called the Black Dot ran by this couple – Marcel Diallo and his wife. They really showed me love and I always will be indebted to Boots for pluggin me into the heart of the Oakland revolution.

By then I had plenty much finished recording at Mr. Laid's spot and now I was just tryin to get the finances to put it out. I talked to Gunny a lot but the old crew in Minnesota was pretty much gone. I was concentrating on the future not lookin back. I had me a cool little apartment not far from downtown San Francisco so I was cool. I still was in the janitorial union so hustlin was far from my mind.

I knew all I had to do was hold on, it was all bout patience now. All the chances I had took to get to this point were bout to pay off just be cool. I kept tellin myself just be cool. I kept my CD player wit me at all times lettin people get a feel of the music, and they was feelin it. It was different. One day Boots called me.

"Fleetwood what's up wit'cha this Boots."

"Oh I'm chillin family how you?"

"Look we gonna have Dead Prez in town on Presidents Day performin and I was wondering did you wanna open up for them?"

"You bullshittin right?"

"N'all fo real."

"Hell yeah Boots fo sho'."

"Cool it's official then."

That night we was sittin in a room in the Marriott wit M1 and stick man from Dead Prez. They had just released that song "It's bigger than Hip Hop." Man these was some cool niggaz. They had heard the song I made for the compilation Boots was puttin out and they liked it. It turned out one of them was from North Carolina, M1, so we bonded real quick. Them niggaz was like fuck the government and wasn't afraid to say it.

You could see it in their eyes and hear it in their voices and just for that you couldn't help but admire them. They were willin to die for what they believed in and what they believed in was black people. These brothas was some modern day warriors in the music business. It was all love. We kicked it for like two days then did the show and I must say we rocked it. Eventually they did pass the Prop 21 law but we put up a helluva fight.

CHAPTER 19

The night after the show I was on the BART headed back to the city and I saw this dude who I had met in JT's studio. His name was J La Rue. This was the cat who wrote Shanice Wilson's album wit Narada Michael Walden. I remember seein him on Arsenio Hall while I was in jail. We chopped it up for awhile.

"La Rue I been at my music still family."

"Is that right Fleet?"

"Fo sho."

"Let me hear something."

I pulled out my CD player, popped in a disk then handed him the headset. His head started noddin immediately, then he looked at me hard as fuck.

"This shit is hella dope, damn my nigga."

"Thanks La Rue."

"Look, who behind you wit this?"

"You know me, I do my own shit."

"This what I want you to do. Go to 1256 3rd St. It's a studio called "Off Planet." Ask for a cat name Bubba Hamp and tell him J La Rue sent you down there."

He gave me the address. The studio was right around the corna from my apartment. The next mornin I rang the buzzer outside the address. The door clicked and I walked into the studio and I couldn't believe how phat it was, it had high ceilings and velvet padded doors that lead into the studios. I informed the receptionist who I was lookin for and she told me were I could find him, told me to go up the stairs to the right and who did I run into on the way up the stairs but JT.

"What you doin in here cuz'n?"

"I came to see Bubba Hamp. J La Rue told me to come down here."

He shook his head. "You a damn hustlin mutha fucka Fleetwood. I'mma show you were he at come on." JT stuck his head in the door.

"Yo bub this my homey Fleetwood. J La rue told him to come holler at you" I walked in the cat office, at the time he was shufflin through some papers. He was a light skinned pimp lookin dude that had danger in his eyes. He stared at me hella hard and I could tell he was readin me. His office had platinum and gold records all on the wall wit a view of the city out the window and I noticed a large framed picture of him wit a cowboy hat on that said "Bubba Hamp for Mayor of San Francisco."

"How you doin sir. My name is Fleetwood. J La Rue told me to come get at'cha."

"Yeah so what's up Fleet? What's own your mind?"

"Well I got some hot music and I'm tryin to find someone to take the time and listen to it and if they like it help me take it to the next level."

"You got it wit you? Put it in the CD player over there."

He didn't even nod his head he just listened. I was gettin nervous and I noticed how he kept on skippin to the next song. Then he started tappin his fingers on the desk a few times.

"Fleet where you from?"

"I'm a west coast country boy, born in the Fillmoe and raised back and forth between North Carolina and here since like the first grade. I been ridin airplanes from coast to coast but when moms died in 1979. I just posted in Cali pretty much."

"Say you from Fillmoe huh?"

"Yeah, my family live in the Bannekers."

"I like your music. It's different and it's hot."

"Thanks sir."

"Man quit callin me sir. My name is Bubba Hamp, call me Bub."

"Alright Bub, I really appreciate you takin out time to listen to my music."

"So what exactly are you tryin to do?"

""I'm tryin to get to the next level."

"Well I'mma be straight up wit you. I can't offer you a big signin bonus to sign wit me but I can get your music out there and put some money in your pocket by ghost writin for people around here in the studio."

"Shit that sound cool to me."

"Right now I'm workin on a Messy Marv album titled Death on a Bitch."

"Yeah I got a song me and Messy and JT and them did back in the day. I never released it."

"If it's tight what you think bout puttin it on the project?"

"Shit that's cool wit me."

We chopped it up for bout like another hour then in walks this old cat that Bubba introduced as Lenny Williams. At the time I didn't know who he was but I later found out he was the legendary Lenny Williams, the one who sung that song "Cause I love you." That night I went home and put my plan together. I was gonna stay as close as I could to Bubba Hamp. Come to find out this was the man who had discovered Sly Stone and managed him back in the day. He also ran for mayor of San Francisco and was elected as a supervisor and had several prominent businesses in the city. He even had a novel out bout his life.

I couldn't believe the situation I was in. I was in the ring wit the heavyweights and I was swinging' like a muthafucka! As the weeks passed I was at the studio every day recording tracks, writin hooks, learnin how to promote albums and whatever they needed me to do. Usually it was Bub, me and Mister – Bub's son. He owned Mega

Entertainment which we ran outta the building and was born wit mack blood in him. He treated me like family from the jump. There was also his youngest son BOBO, the next Barry Bonds, and his two nephews Marvelous Marv and J-Stone. Me and Bub bonded and he knew he could count on me for whatever.

One day I came in the studio and it was this old dude sittin to the side wit some colored strings all in his hair. I'm like "who is that" and that's when Messy came out one of the rooms of the studio and pulled me to the side he was like – "Fleet you know who that is?"

"N'all who the fuck is that crazy lookin nigga wit all that string and shit in his head?"

'Nigga that's Clinton" said Messy.

"Clinton who?"

"George Clinton boy!"

"Fo real? I be damn! Sho is, damn!"

Here I was in the lab wit the funk master himself, Mr. George Clinton. Mess had came back up from down south to work on this project and Bub had called Clinton to do some tracks. For the next two days we were in that studio and I left once, I think I went home once to change clothes. It was amazin to see this master of funk and I learned so much from just watchin him. His work ethic was what I gained the most. He was non stop recording. He kept sayin this shit cost money, don't waste your time when you get in here Fleetwood. I never forget that. Every now and then I would sneak in a freestyle wit Mess but my vocals never made it to the project. Shit, I didn't give a fuck! I was like a Acura dealer – surrounded by Legends.

After Clinton finished his work, Messy went back down south and we continued to get the album ready. Off Planet had a phat website that this cat name Sergio had created. I let him hear my music from Minnesota "Probable Cause." Him and Bub convinced the people at the studio to put my album out through the website first which I had no problem at all wit.

One day I went to go holler at my partner Bizzy Ben at his Straight Forward office and who do I see but Lenny Williams. Come to find out this is where Lenny did some community activist work. I had wrote this song "Institutionalized" bout a week earlier. I let Bizzy hear the lyrics and he loved it. It was something I could perform out in the community and at schools.

"Lenny, Fleetwood got this song" said Bizzy, walkin over to Lenny. "He want you to sing on it. It's hot."

"Let me hear what the lyrics sound like." Before I was halfway through the first verse I had him.

"No problem, I like that. But I'll need a point off your album if it's released major."

"Cool I ain't got no problem wit that."

I knew the studio at Off Planet was booked for the next three days so I called Mr. Laid and told him the situation. The next night we was at the spot wit Mr. Laid and Chill Black, doin our thang. Lenny went into the booth and I just had him singin "I'm institutionalized. I'm tired of being locked up. They ain't gonna never let me go." At first I was tryin to coach him and Mr. Laid nudged me like nigga let him do him. I had forgot this man had recorded one of the biggest love songs ever so we just sat back and listened to greatness. It was amazing. I think it took him like twenty minutes and he stacked the vocals like eight times. It was a wrap, one of the best moments I ever had in the studio and to this day "Institutionalized" is one of the hottest songs I ever made.

After we finish the song I was amped so I went straight to Off Planet to let Bubba hear it. When I told him I had Lenny on a song he got a strange look on his face because he knew I hadn't been in the studio wit him while he was there.

"It's a tight song. To be honest wit you Fleet that's gonna be a classic."

"Thanks Bub."

"But let me explain something to ya. It was disrespectful for you to go somewhere else and do a song wit someone I introduced you to at this studio."

"But the studio was locked down."

"But Fleet you didn't give me the chance to unlock it. See, fo my family I'll do anything and Fleet you family."

At first I didn't understand why he was hot at me.

"See one thing bout this game you will come to learn: it's hella scandalous and loyalty is something you rarely find."

"Bub I'll never cross you."

"I know you won't, that's why you sittin right there and I'm explainin this to ya."

"Fo sho."

"But what I want you to understand is that I fucked wit you from the jump because you was humble and hungry, not because you had talent or that Messy song. I can get that shit anywhere you understand?"

"Most definitely Bub."

He reminded me to not get big headed and I understood. A few days passed and everything was cool again. At the same time it was a major street war jumpin off in the Hunter's Point neighborhood in the big maze of projects between West Mob, where Larceny and Hectic was from, and a crew who was on Harbor Rd. who had a label called Big Block that had just got a major distribution deal.

Now I use to fuck wit them Harbor Rd. niggaz back in the days – Flop, Nard Tiger, Chuck (RIP), African Ed, December, Dougie Fresh and Big Ben. Them niggaz put me on as a youngsta. But now it was a new generation and I was wit Hectic and Larceny almost everyday, comin to pick them up and droppin them off in the heart of the West Mob. The two turfs where right around the corner from each other and the shit was real crazy.

Niggaz was gettin killed everyday, it was definitely gettin out of control. At the same time my homey from the West Mob block, Kevin Epps, was makin a documentary bout the whole situation called "Straight Outta Hunter's Point," my film debut, it went on to win many awards.

Anyway, Bub told me one day it wasn't cool to be up there like that. My car had already been mentioned in the wrong type of way and like I said people were droppin. So I explained to Larceny and Hectic I would have to meet them some other place. At the time Midnite Blu was dealin wit some issues and she decided rap was secondary. She stopped comin around and eventually moved to Portland. So now I had this Minimum Wage project and I didn't really know what to do wit it. One day I went to Off Planet and talked to Bub.

"Look Fleet these muthafuckas done decided they wanna go in another direction."

"What you mean Bub?"

"They say this rap shit ain't where they wanna put their money. They gonna concentrate on movie scores and animation."

Shit it was all bad. We had just released the Messy project and here this shit happens.

"This the type of shit that happens in this game Fleet. You never know. One minute you up, the next you back to strugglin. That's why it's important to treat everyone the same because you never know who will blow and you might need a favor" he said, lookin me straight in my eyes.

So we moved outta "Off Planet". The street shit was gettin worse. A couple cats close to me got smoked and I had had enough. I needed a break from California.

CHAPTER 20

So come to find out Sergio the computer genius was from Minnesota and he had a RV headed back in a few days. I called Gunny and he was happy as fuck and told me to come back. So I told Bub.

"Bub I'm bout to go back to Minnesota for awhile, this shit gettin a little too crazy for me."

"Yeah Fleet these niggaz ain't got shit to live for, that's why they don't give a fuck bout killin you or doin life in prison."

"Bub don't forget bout me now. I'll be back."

"Fleet that's one thing you don't ever have to worry bout and that's your spot on the team. You always got that."

I told Larceny and Hectic I was leavin. They didn't like it but they understood. Within 24 hours I was on the highway headed back to Minnesota. The only thing I was thinkin bout was stayin out the penitentiary and the grave yard. I knew I had plugs and my plan was to just lay low till the smoke cleared and go back to Cali. It was 1999. I guess this what Prince was singin bout back then, feel me? Drama all over the hood. We finally arrived and Sergio dropped me off at Fancy's house.

"Who is it?"

"It's Fleetwood."

"Fleetwood! Momma look it's Floyd! When you get here?"

"Shit I just got back up here. I just got off the highway, my man dropped me off."

"Who" she said as she looked out the door and saw this big azz RV.

"That's my partna Sergio."

"Oh okay, so how long you gonna stay?"

"I don't know Fancy. Look though, I need somewhere to crash until I can get my paper up. You think your moms will let me crash here?"

"Boy you know you family! You better quit playin." She hugged me hella tight.

"Fleetwood I'm so glad you here now I know shit bout to be straight."

I hooked back up wit Gunny and Looney G and Robdog. We went in the studio and did some shit. It was cool but the same beef I had left in Cali was poppin' off just as hard in Minnesota. Niggaz was at war. After bout a week I moved in wit this female. It didn't take 3 weeks before I came to her crib and all my shit was on the porch.

"What the fuck is my shit doin out here?" I'm screamin through the screen as she stands her thick azz there wit her hands on her hips.

"Where the fuck this rubber come from?"

"What rubber?"

"That rubber that was in your jeans."

"Man I don't know what the fuck you talkin bout."

"Well don't worry bout it you ain't got to worry bout me sweatin you no more" she said, slammin the door shut in my face. I was bout to kick the door in. Thank GOD for better judgment.

So now a nigga was homeless in Minnesota. I had to eat so I went back to the block and eventually went to jail for lurkin wit intent like three times. The last time I was like "fuck this." I got back on a Greyhound and headed back to Cali. When I touch down the shit was all in the paper, all on the evening news: it was a war in the streets it won't safe. So I called my cousin Terry down south.

"You need to bring your black azz back down here before something crazy happen" he said.

"Nigga I just got shit goin good. I got my album on the internet, I'm in a documentary out there. I got real connects now cuz'n."

"But what good is it if you won't be around to enjoy it? You gotta give yourself a chance to breathe."

"I feel ya but my ends fucked up."

"I got you don't worry bout shit."

So here I go back on a Greyhound headed to the Dirty South, thinkin bout the studio, Off Planet being closed, the wars in the streets of Hunters Point and Minnesota, the connects I had obtained, the love I had wit Bub. Shit, I knew I had left a lot behind me but I also knew I needed a break. I was burnt out really. I had a lot of unresolved issues wit my mother's side of the family that I knew I would have to deal wit. Shit I wasn't really even tryin to discuss. After three long days on the bus I got to North Carolina. My cousin Terry came and picked me up. It was good to see him. He was always like my brother, that's how we had grew up. Anyway, I got settled in and it was all good.

That night we went to a strip club. Man, had North Carolina changed since I left. It was black strip clubs everywhere. Females I had went to school wit that was super square was now shakin that azz fast for the cash. To be honest it was the first time I really had been in a strip club and my tolerance was very low as far as dealin wit their trickery. Shit, that night I tried to holler at every stripper in my path and got hella disgusted when I got the usual run around that they give. I started wildin' in the joint, throwin pennies on the stage and shit. Just stupid shit. Terry eventually got me up outta there but I could feel the Cali wildness comin out.

As the days passed Terry lent me his truck and I went out lookin for work. One night I got drunk as hell and I saw a breezy walkin down the street. Wasn't payin attention and ran off the road, fucked up my cousin truck. That nigga was hot. By then I had developed a drinkin problem. I woke up drinkin beer and went to sleep drunk. I was just burnt out on the rap game. I just tried to drink myself stupid to hide the pain and disappointment of what had happen wit the music. After a while my cousin had enough an told me I had to move. He had love for me, I knew that, but I was on some destructive shit. My other cousin Rick Goins who was a barber took me in.

"You can come live wit us in the basement."

"You think it'll be cool?"

"Yeah but I'mma tell ya Rob. I ain't havin that bullshit in my house."

"I gotcha Rick. I gotcha."

So here was an opportunity for me to get my thoughts together and pretty much just figure out what I was gonna do. For like nine months all I did was watch TV, eat and sleep. I didn't want to fuck wit that rap shit at all. It had brought so much bullshit into my life I was like "fuck the rap game." My cousin's son Laric kept sayin "big cousin get back at your music." I just wasn't feelin it but I was good to hear someone believe in me.

I hadn't talked to Bub now in damn near a year and every now and then I would see a rap magazine and see how JT and Messy were makin moves on the independent scene. I was happy for them but mad as fuck at myself because I knew I was suppose to be right there wit them. This shit only frustrated me even more.

CHAPTER 21

One night I was sittin round flippin' through the channels and I stopped on this local show bout social change. It was this dude hosting named Timothy X and he kept sayin "if you don't like my show come down here and start your own." His show was called "CMP Live" – See My Perspective live. It was 2001 now and I had really been hibernating in my cousin's basement damn near a year now. I knew it was time to make my move. I called the television station the next mornin.

"Hello GCTV."

"Yes I'm callin bout how to go bout startin a television show on your channel."

"Well first you need to set up an appointment and come to the orientation sir."

"That's what I would like to do. When is the next one?"

"Tomorrow actually."

The next day I was down there goin through the orientation process. I couldn't believe these people was bout to let me be on TV for free for an hour a week. It was only one problem though. I needed to learn how to edit my show. The classes started in three weeks and took four weeks to complete, so that meant I would have to wait almost two months for my first show to air. I wasn't feelin that shit. That's when I met this cat in the station named Curtis Muhammed. He was in the Nation of Islam and I could tell by his mannerisms and attire, something I picked up just from being in prison wit Muslims. I noticed he was fuckin wit the editing equipment and it really seemed like he knew what he was doin.

"Say brotha it seems like you really know what you're doin wit that editing."

"Yeah I kinda got a handle on it."

"Look I just started my show and I'm lookin fo someone to help edit it fo me. Would you be interested brotha?"

"Most definitely, if you could compensate me for it, it wouldn't be no problem."

"How much you gonna charge me?"

"We'll work it out, maybe $20 a show."

"Cool I can handle that."

I had my first show on the air within a week. At the time there was another video show on the station but it was more New York focused. I based my show around southern and west coast groups and independent videos, givin them the shine denied by the major TV networks. I titled my show "The Dirty Dirty" and for the first couple of weeks, maybe like three shows, I never appeared on screen, only my voice. I really wasn't tryin to be on TV, I was concentrating on establishing connections in the music game.

This is how I learned to use a computer. I went to the library everyday, started wit an email address and just kept playin wit it. Before I knew it I was on the phone wit Rap a Lot Records' video promotion department. They were the first label to show me love, then I got wit all the major independents. UPS was comin to my cousin's house like every other day droppin off videos for me to play. After bout a month and a half I heard Ludacris was comin to town.

North Carolina is a college hot bed so entertainers frequent the area to break new acts. I was all hyped bout interviewing Ludacris. I went to meet him to holler at him but I hadn't got it cleared through

Def Jam so I couldn't. This was my first lesson in the TV game. See you had to always have a contact to interview people, most of the time it was the artist's manager. So the next day I called Def Jam's video promotion department. They asked me how many people I was reachin and how long my show had been up and what was it's purpose. I explained to them what I was doin in North Carolina and after I got off the phone I had a plug wit Def Jam, it was official. Now I could interview anyone from their label that came to North Carolina.

Basically I was just watchin BET and MTV and doin the opposite of what they were doin as far as major programmin, commercials and showin major acts. I still followed how they interviewed people and their techniques. I watched their posture and how they held the mics shit like that, as well as how to format the show. When it came to promotin what I did was include the hood. I put niggaz on TV cause I knew that they would have their people watchin. That was the next best thing to a commercial, like "watch my shit, feel me? You gonna be on it." And basically what I did was go to stores and see what the underground artist labels were and then called their city and hollered at the video promotion people. Before I knew it the word got around in the underground there was a new video show in North Carolina called "The Dirty Dirty," get them videos asap, real talk.

I had startin gettin a bunch of Luke videos from Miami and I was playin them wit no problem until one night I showed like three of these old school videos – booty poppin' shit. The following mornin I get a call.

"May I speak to Fleetwood" the woman on the other end said.

"Yeah this him, who this?"

"This is Ms. Logan from GCTV. Have you seen the newspaper this mornin?"

"No I haven't."

"Well you and your TV show made the front page. You are officially a celebrity."

"Is that right? Imagine that. Well thank you for callin and you have a nice day."

What had happen was that a lady had seen like three minutes of the show surfin through the channels and she caught one of the Luke video's and felt that the women dancing were simulating sex. She got so upset she called the newspaper, the city council and anyone that would listen. But the whole hype was that I had did everything appropriately, by havin my show come on after 1 AM and havin a parental advisory disclaimer appear before my show came on. So I had covered my azz and all this lady did was blow my show up. My phone started ringin off the hook and everyone wanted to know who was this new dude in town behind "The Dirty Dirty."

The next day I was scheduled to appear on the radio on the hottest mornin show in the region – a very controversial show hosted by Busta Brown, Peaches – Ms. Superbad herself, and Amos Quick – known for puttin people on the spot. But I knew I could handle it and I knew it would give me the opportunity to tell my side of the story and besides this was free exposure that I couldn't pass up. Busta Brown was suppose to be a hard azz but I found out he was from Cali, San Francisco at that, so I knew when he found out I was from the bay it would be all good.

I rode to the station wit two Muslim's from the nation – brotha Soleed and Curtis Muhammed. These brothas really embraced me, much love to them both and their cause. The first person I see is Peaches' fine azz. Now she was a southern bell for real – red bone, pretty, country and smart – just my type. But I was there for business and I kept that in mind. I walked over and shook hands wit Amos Quick then Busta.

"What's up Busta how you doin fam?"

"How you doin Amos."

"Dirty Dirty! What's goin on man? They got you all on the front page what's up wit that brotha?"

"Well you know I grew up lookin guilty so it don't really surprise me none."

"So Fleet you from California, huh?"

"Yeah the Bay, Fillmoe to be exact."

"You know I'm from The Point?"

"Yeah I was told that, that's why I brought these pictures wit me."

"Damn, I be damn yo, this HP! You is from the Sco. huh?"

"I told'cha Bust, I grew up in the Bay and the Cackalacky, feel me?"

He couldn't believe the pictures from the hood. We did the interview and I ran my mouth real decent. After bout three questions all the phones lit up. It was no secret now, a new celeb was in town. I got motivational speakin offers, all kinds of people thinkin I could sign them and just a gang of people wanted to be down wit what I was doin. And that's when all the bullshit started.

The next day I go to the station and get a funny vibe from the VJ from the other video show. Their show had been up for like four years and never got that much exposure. I could understand but that was on them not me. That same day I met wit this intern and told him he could come work on the show. Around this time I startin airing the segment of the show called "Listen to my Demo" where me and the intern would go out in the hood and film people rappin right in their element. The shit was dope, it brought the youth of the streets to the screen.

CHAPTER 22

Anyway my intern had some homeys so I started workin wit them. The first was Lil Black. He was my intern's partner, a local gunslinger wit plenty of sticky. He had the look, the voice and the rhymes. He knew he was dope and I knew he was dope but I also knew he was in the streets. I knew it was gonna be risky fuckin wit him. Shit could go on pause at any moment but I felt something bout the dude, I just hoped and prayed I could get him a deal before the game caught him up, feel me? The cat was so talented it was crazy, I really didn't have the funds to have the lil nigga stop hustlin and he had kids so I just prayed for the best and expected the worst.

I met two other youngstas from different parts of the city – a girl from St. Louis' south side named "Pretty Thug" and "Third Rail" – he lived on the east side and his brotha Jesse was like the first DJ and rapper in the city. I remembered him from when I was down there as a shorty. Then it was this one cat named King Hussein I met him on the block. One day I was gettin some gas and heard this nigga rappin hella fast when I walked over and listened closely to him I realized he was freestylin. Now a lotta niggaz can freestyle, but fast? That's a gifted person, so after he finished I asked him to be down wit us. It was that easy, he said hell yeah and it was on. I got them all together one day.

"How y'all feel bout startin a group?"

We sat at the park. It was Lil Black, Pretty Thug, King Hussein, Third Rail and Me.

"Shit, I'm wit it Fleet" said Lil Black.

"Wood that shit sound good to me" said King Hussein.

"Fleetwood you the only one that really ever showed us any love. We ridin wit whatever you wanna do" Pretty Thug said and Third Rail agreed. So it was official, I had me a group again. I was startin to get that feelin back.

"What y'all think bout The Foundation as a name?"

Everyone thought it was dope, so there it was. The whole time I had been goin around town hollering at different businesses to see if they would sponsor my show. So I hollered at a couple of studios and one was down to trade recording time for advertising on the show. The name of the studio was ESC – Every Second Counts – ran by Lamar and Jerrell Crump. Jerrell ran the boards and he also was producing this girl at the time – an R&B singer.

Immediately I started recording wit The Foundation every weekend. The show was more popular every week and I was out regularly, anywhere anything was poppin I'd be there. One day I found out Master P would be in North Carolina and I immediately called Universal and arranged an interview. I had a female on the show, "Famous," to help me host for a new flava.

I couldn't believe I was bout to meet the same cat that I had listened to over and over in the penitentiary, I had come a long way fast and I had one goal: to get as much game from this cat as possible. I knew he could teach me a lot, it was just bout approaching him in the right way. This was the new Barry Gordy of music and I couldn't wait to holler at him. When we got there we had to wait like an hour but finally we saw him arrive wit Lil Romeo. We were standing right outside of their dressing room.

What's up brotha. You Greg Lyons?" I said to the dude security had told me to holla at.

"Yes, who are you?"

"My name is Fleetwood from the 'Dirty Dirty' TV show. I spoke to ya earlier."

"Oh yeah what's up Fleet. How you doin?"

"Man I'm cool, just waitin to holla at P."

"Let me go in and make sure they're settled then I'll be back out to get y'all."

"Cool." After bout ten minutes, Greg reappeared.

"Y'all ready Fleet?" Greg said in a way like "You family homey," which was cool.

"Most definitely."

I wasn't really nervous, more anxious. As we walked in the first thing I noticed was the jewels Lil Romeo had on his bracelet. It had to be worth $100,000 alone.

"What's up P, how you doin family" I asked.

"What goin on Dirty?"

"This my co-host 'Famous' right here."

"Hello, how you doin Famous?"

"Hi pleasure to meet you. You think we could get Romeo to join us?" She did it right on point. I was caught up in gettin as much game as I could from P.

"Rom come mere for a minute" Master P called him over and he was sat a few seats away from us wit his dancers.

"What's up Rom how you doin Lil homey?"

"I'm cool. I'm cool"

"I just wanna tell ya I'm very proud of you."

"Thanks man, thank you very much."

I let Famous ask a few questions then I took over the interview.

"Dirty where you from" P asked.

"I was born in Fillmoe, CA and raised between there and North Carolina" I told him.

"Is that right? So you from the Bay huh? I knew it was something bout you."

"P, I remember when you came out wit "Mama's Bad Boy" and had your shit on all the bus stops, fuckin wit funky phat before anybody."

"You remember huh?"

"Yeah, you was the first one I ever seen that advertised your next album inside your album cover."

"A lotta people don't give me my due but I ain't trippin Fleet."

"Man the bay got a lotta love for ya."

"You know that's home for me, say Fleet you know JT?"

"Yeah Figgaro the homey."

"So what, you doin this TV thang huh?"

"Well I'm usin it as a vehicle to get inside the industry."

"That's smart my nigga, that's smart. Look, whatever I can do let me know" Master P said.

"Fo sho'. Look, I'mma let you go I know you got a busy schedule. I love homey."

"Fo sho' Fleet. Get at me" P said.

After we finished talkin he gave me a number to get at him through Uncle Greg. To this day the number is good. He was one of the coolest down to earth cats I ever met in the rap game. This was definitely a highlight in my VJ career.

In the following months I would interview the likes of Styles P from the Lox, Sharissa, Jaheim, Nappy Roots, the Clipse, NORE and Capone, Lady May, Midwikit, Rob Jackson and the following week I had a big interview wit Cam'ron. This was the beginning of Dip Set and he was blowin up. I had been havin trouble at the station because the program director kept fuckin wit me. Also there was inside hatin from the rival show. One day I went to the station.

"Mr. Bowden can we speak to you for a minute" the director said as I walked past his desk.

"Yeah what's goin on?"

"Well I looked at your show and there's some very questionable behavior that we can't allow on the station."

"What you talkin bout now man?"

"Well you have women dancing and simulating sex."

"What? Man what you talkin bout? Y'all just tryin to find a way to shut me down but you know what? I'll edit out whatever you think is wrong."

"Well Mr. Bowden, unfortunately it's past the deadline to turn in your show so if you do edit it, it will be too late to be seen this week."

"Oh this the slick part huh? The paper work."

"Excuse me, can you leave my office please. Our discussion is finished."

"You called me in here and I can't finish what I have to say huh?"

"I'm asking you again can you please leave my office." He was hella nervous and startin to sweat.

"I want to know why I wasn't contacted earlier so I could correct the editing of my show."

We went back and forth a few times. I never threatened the guy or used profanity but before I knew it the police were there and they told the police I was intimidating and needed to leave. Two days later I received a letter sayin I was banned from the station and my show would be canceled. They thought I was fucked. All I did was change the name of the show to "On the Porch" and had my intern register it in his name. The show never missed a beat. I couldn't go to the station so I started editing the show at home wit two VCR's and a pause button. By this time Famous was gone and I had a new cameraman named Yusef Malik, a real good conscious brotha. The Foundation had recorded almost ten songs and we had one song gettin spins on the mix shows. The buzz was growin and the music was leakin to the streets. Everybody and they mama was watchin and talkin bout my show. What I did was involve the community. I stayed in the projects, puttin the lil homeys on TV. I had every label in the industry hittin me now because I had an audience of over a 100,000 people watchin me every Friday night. I couldn't be denied, feel me?

Finally the time came to interview Cam'ron. We interviewed him backstage after the show.

"What's up homey? You got the whole world screamin Oh Boy."

"Yeah it's a blessin."

"You came along way from Horse and a Carriage."

"Most definitely, this whole situation, the rap game is nothin but a hustle. It's based on consistency you know."

"Well you definitely doin your thang."

"Oh I see you doin your thing too."

"Well you know... tryin to find my way in that's all."

"Ay peace to everybody down in North Carolina. Dip Set got love fo ya and make sure y'all keep that shit locked on my man here "On Da Porch" TV Show."

I was surprised at how humble he was. He had a hit record and it was like it was nothin. Before he left he told me how much he appreciated me and I've always supported Dip Set from then on. The show had a few kinks here and there but basically we kept it in motion. They knew it was me behind the show but they couldn't do shit bout it. The Foundation was doin good, we were performin all over the city and they was really feelin us. My cousin Terry threw annual bike rallies and he always let us rock. They were off the hook and he had one comin up and "Sunshine Anderson" was performin. Sunshine was fine and sexy as hell. I must say I got kinda nervous but I rolled wit it during the interview and it came off smooth. The next week I got wit Juelz Santana. He was a real hustla, reminded me of LP in Minnesota.

Around the same time I started havin trouble wit The Foundation. Pretty Thug was bout to have a baby, then some street shit happened wit her dude and they went back to St. Louis. Third Rail was havin problems wit his PO and it caused so much stress he told me he needed a break from the game. I understood but I also understood we had to keep movin. Even though we had took pictures and all we would have to do it all over, fuck it. It was 2002 now and Lil Black was still down wit me. I had my homey Pap Smooth rollin wit us and the only thing I knew to do was keep on makin connects. By now I had real numbers and relationships in every major label and the big independents. This was when I met the Youngbloods. We did the interview and when we was leavin I started singin one of my crunk hooks. Mark Twain was their producer at the time and later that night he came up to me at the after party.

"Yo what's up Fleet."

"I'm chillin Twain, y'all straight?"

"Yeah we cool. Looka here, that hook you was singin earlier comin out the club, was that y'all shit?"

"Yeah that's one of my hooks. That's all I do is write hooks all day."

"Ay I like that shit. What you think bout comin down to the A and fuckin wit us?"

"Man you bullshittin right?"

"N'all my nigga. When we get off tour I want you to come to the studio and I'mma see what you can do."

At the time they were on a world tour wit Lil John and the Eastside Boyz and had that hit record "Damn" He gave me a number to stay in touch wit them while they where on the road. I was gettin close now and I could feel it. So could people around me. From that moment on all I did was stay at my partna 7blowz house on the south side, writin crunk hooks.

CHAPTER 23

7blowz was this dude I met through "listen to my demo." He was a hot rapper/producer from South Carolina and within the next two years we would become like brothers. He's a member of the production team I still deal wit call "the Breakfast club." I was livin in a big Victorian house my auntie in New York owned that was formerly a boardin house. It was located by the campus of N.C. A&T so I was surrounded by a non stop shuffle of college students.

It was a Bp gas station up the street and if I wasn't in the studio, this is where you could find me. This was how I survived. I had quit fuckin wit the crack game completely so I sold CD's out front. I usta honestly make around one hundred dollars in like four or five hours a day wit no sweat from the police so it was cool. At the store I did plenty of networkin and during homecoming week it was off the hook. What black colleges brought to the rap game was priceless, this was an atmosphere that you could find educated, young, wild crowds. You felt like lettin loose but also felt like they had something to lose. The first thang I noticed bout the black college crowd was there was hardly any riots at the shows, some fights but never random violence. Nobody gettin killed and shit. So artists came through on the regular, feel me? It was nothin to have two shows wit big name artist in the same week. It's just a completely different vibe down south.

I had an interview wit "3 Six Mafia" comin up that I was really hyped bout. These were some wild cats and I definitely enjoyed their music. That same week Lil Black got locked up and I knew then it was time for me to start recording solo songs so no matter what I could perform and keep things goin.

Around this time is when I met my partna "Now Un" from New Jersey. He was in the promotions game and just a real good brotha. We hung out everyday hustlin CD's, promotin the show and vibin at 7blowz house. Now Un introduced me to this cat Jerz, who made beats. He had a brotha named Kareem who ran D&D Promotions. We started doin a lot of work together and Kareem helped me out a lot on the show. To this day he's a very good friend. The whole time the show was still goin on and I did interviews wit David Banner (a good brotha), Chingy and Funk Master Flex. It was the summer of 2002 and I was doin good.

We kept doin shows, me and Lil Black, Pap Smooth and sometimes Now Un. My auntie now had moved back from New York to help take care of my grandmother who was gettin sick. It was a big difference wit her being there but I adapted and as the months passed I continued to hustle CD's and make music. I had a few breezies and thangs was cool. I knew all I had to do was be patient and keep connecting, my time was comin.

I called Mark Twain every now and then to make sure they wouldn't forget bout me but I knew it would be awhile. They were on a world tour now wit Lil John. I just kept grindin and fuckin wit 7blowz everyday. Lil Black would come through sometimes but we never really hung out like that. It was gettin close to the end of the year now and really I was gettin tired of the TV show. Being on TV comes wit a lotta hate, plus I was gettin tired of not being able to go no where without people knowin who I was. I started isolatin myself more and more.

2003 rolled in wit new vision, ideas, possibilities and interviews. At the studio Jerrell Crump kept tellin me "Fleetwood you the nigga. Outta all them cats you brought in here the shit you do is the hottest."

Jerrell and Lamar really believed in me and Lamar had some hot tracks so I was like "fuck it." Every chance I got I would record a solo song for my own project. I did a song wit this girl named Baby Luv called "Only 1" dedicated to my mother. I was performin this song now at a lotta parks and community centers gettin good feedback.

Round this time I started hangin in strip clubs and they were everywhere. It was one spot you could find me at regularly called Twiggleys. I wanted to develop a relationship so I could eventually have the dancers dance to my songs, this was my intentions, but like any other man around a bunch of naked azz women all the time I started slippin, gettin too personal. I started likin a few of them knowin that they bout money that's it. Down south it's nothin to see females you went to school wit gettin naked and dancing. That's not countin all the college girls who dance to try to make it. The shit never stops.

New strippers every week, every day. A new nightclub opened, just a regular club no strippin, and I had an agreement wit the promoter to put it on TV for a fee. This is really when I began to deal wit DJ's from the radio station, around the same time. I had recorded a single called "That's What's Up" and it was gettin good feedback in the streets. So I was tryin to get it on the radio so this would be like a win win situation, feel me? A way to get in wit them. I'd been showin them on TV from time to time so they showed me love back. Captain J was a mix show DJ that took a likin to what I was doin.

"Say bro my name Capt J. I'm feelin your shit homey fo real."

"Thanks man" I told him. "I really I appreciate that comin from someone who be on the radio."

"This my number. If it's something I can do fo ya get at me. I gotcha."

Before he left he told me he would always support me. That was rare in the radio game.

CHAPTER 24

D.J. Coyote worked at the radio station and owned a label himself. He was a cool dude from Palestine who came over for college and started hustlin in the rap game. Me and this dude got close and our crews had a lotta mutual respect. This cat and the station's program director Tap Money showed me a lotta love. Tap was a real down to earth African homey who I still reach out to from time to time.

Lil Flip was comin up at the time and I had an interview comin up wit him. He had that smash hit record out "Game Over" and was doin his thang so I was definitely lookin to plug in wit them Texas boys. Bout the same time I'd also met this youngsta Lil Walt who was hot wit the Fruity Loops program makin beats, so me and him started hangin out a lot. We made like 12 songs in a week – hot ones. The magic was there and I took him wit me to meet Lil Flip. We let em hear some of our shit.

"Damn family that shit hot, is it on the street?" asked Flip standing by his boy. They were both noddin their heads.

"N'all" I told em. "We bout to put it out though."

"Look write this number down. I want y'all to fuck wit us."

"Flip all I do is write hooks, family, I really ain't tryin to be no rapper no more."

"Shit that's what we lookin fo my nigga."

"Yo, you say you from the bay right? You know Cellski?"

"Yeah that's the homey."

"You know I fucks wit him real tough."

"Is that right? You bullshittin!"

"N'all so you see we gotta link."

"Most definitely I'mma call y'all."

I knew an easy way into the game was writin hooks so that's how I always came at people. I was gettin too old to be still rappin in many people eyes, so I mastered the art of hook writin and I knew it would get me in. Flip told me don't lose the number and to stay in touch. Right after that I got back in touch wit Bubba Hamp and sent him a copy of my show. He was proud of his protégé.

"Fleet you doin your thang boy. I told you a long time ago you was a winner."

"I'm just doin what my OG's like you taught me Bub."

"Look Fleet you know I'm out here in Vegas. I want you to come see me."

"When?"

"Shit you can come tomorrow if you want my nigga. Find out how much the ticket cost and call me back."

I had got a message from my homeboy Kevin Epps in Cali sayin he'd finished his documentary "Straight Outta Hunters Point" and had me in it. He said he'd be at Duke University in a few weeks and wanted to know if I wanted to come to the screenin and perform at the after party. I couldn't believe it. So me, Lil Black, 7blowz, BeBe and Kareem went down to Duke. The documentary was off the hook and we rocked the after party. Thangs in the streets of San Francisco was gettin real dangerous and my homey Kev caught the essence on film.

A week passed and I got a call from my cousin Terry sayin our little cousin Jeffery Bracken a.k.a. Fizzle had got killed. It was a sad day for the family. Fizzle was a good young man but fell victim to society's war on drugs. The day of the funeral I woke up late and when I finally got to the church the place was packed.

I sat in the back and listened to the preacher as everyone in the family cried. I couldn't take it any longer. I got up, walked past the casket then left the church. I walked all the way home and by the time I got there I had the lyrics to song "Fizzle." That night I called Jerrell Crump and we dropped it. To this day its a slapper.

After a while I really started to feel like "fuck this TV show" and "fuck these labels." It had got to the point where they were callin me demandin me to play there videos. I realized the only reason they were pluggin me wit interviews was to promote their artists, so I began askin for paper for street team promotions. It worked out for a few labels but the majority were offering pennies. I needed more connects so I kept the communication lines open, but really the love was fadin.

It was late summer now and my grandmother was gettin sicker and stayin at the house wit us. My auntie kept an eye on her but we were startin to have differences that would eventually clash. But she supported me through all my struggles and I'll always love her for that.

Lately I'd been spending a lot of time at ESC wit Jerrell Crump. Lamar gave me some beats and I was just droppin songs solo. I had recorded two songs, one called "The Country" and the other one "Ghetto Holiday" and my man Jerz had gave me a beat for a song called "That's What's Up" that was already gettin good feedback. All these were me solo. Even though I was concentrating on writin hooks I still wasn't gonna stop rappin, never that. When I finished the vocals they knew it and so did I: we had made some monsters. All I needed to make them hit records was money for promoting and marketing. So I called my cousin Terry.

"T what up cuz'n."

"What you you want nigga?"

"Man I done made that bomb boy! I got us one, I just need some backin."

"Nigga you always say that shit when you come out the studio."

"I'm tellin your big head azz this a hit record."

"Let me hear the shit."

"Now take in mind this over the phone."

"Nigga just play the shit."

I let it bump for bout two minutes. "What you think?"

"Nigga that shit slammin! What you talkin bout you need?"

"We gotta get posters, airplay, all kinda shit."

"Nigga meet me at Unc's house in two hours."

"I told'cha it was a hit nigga."

"Bout time, all the muthafuckin time you spend in that bitch."

We met up and he gave me what I needed to press up some singles. People in the streets was feelin it then Captain J started playin it on the radio and within a few weeks I had like 10 radio stations bumpin it down south. The buzz was growin. At the same time Lil Black was catchin cases and was in and outta jail. I could hear the desperation in his voice. He had to get on fast before he got locked. I had an interview wit Scarface comin up that I was really lookin forward to. I'd been a fan of the Geto Boys since the beginning so I couldn't wait to sit down and talk to Brad Jordan.

The day came and I went wit Clos – a dope hungry young rapper that rhymed wit my homey Tec in a group called Lost Minds. They always showed me love and vice versa. We rode hard together and still do. They worked wit Ski Beats who had produced a lot of tracks on Jay-Z's first album. Scarface walked in and went straight to the bar. He did an interview wit this dude from Virginia and after they finished I hollered at the contact from Def Jam.

"Yo man what's up? When I'mma get to do my interview?"

"I'm sorry Fleetwood" the rep said. "He said he was finish fo the day."

I knew my contact wasn't frontin on me but that didn't mean I was gonna quit. I walked up to Scarface.

'Yo man I got the dopest TV show in the south. I need to interview you."

"Is that right that's what that last nigga said."

'I'm from the block Face. Hustlas and gangstas watch my shit. I don't know what that man show bout but mine from the gangsta's perspective, feel me?"

"What's your name partna?"

"They call me Fleetwood."

"Fleetwood I fucks wit niggaz like you. What you need from me?"

Scarface and I must have talked for bout an hour. This wasn't no dumb nigga and he gave me all kinds of advice bout the game. More importantly, he hollered at me bout life and I really appreciated that. I'll always have love for him for that. A few weeks passed and it was the beginning of November. One night at the house I woke to screams from my auntie. I thought I was dreamin but I wasn't.

"Robert! Robert come downstairs!" she kept hollering.

"What's wrong aunt Barbara?" I asked, scramblin to get my clothes on.

"Momma"s dead! Momma's dead!!!!"

I dropped my head and went and hugged my auntie.

It was all bad. My mother's mother was gone. I had to go downstairs and face my grandmother, lyin there dead wit her eyes open. Standing in that room waitin on the grave diggers all I could think bout was how many collect phone calls from prison she'd accepted, all the obstacles she had told me that I would have to deal wit and her strong spirit. For days I was in a daze. My mother's family were all in town. It was such a phony situation. I'd never really bonded wit most of them before and now was no different. Death brings out the greed in a family quick. Knowin money was comin from the blood of my grandmother, the vultures were circlin. It was sad to sit back and watch.

After the funeral was over everyone went back home and there was a strange feelin in that house. I just didn't feel comfortable there anymore. One day I was talkin to my cousin Romona who was a school teacher in Washington DC.

"Robert I heard what you been doin down there. Why don't you come and talk to my students in DC?"

"For real? When?"

"When can you come?"

"Set it up and I'll be there."

I was wit it. Reaching out and sharing my life experiences fed my soul. I was hopin it would help someone else avoid the pitfalls I'd fell into. Plus I needed a break, so this was perfect. I did some research on who her students were and discovered that there was the younger brother of the kid from the HBO documentary "Thug life in DC" an acclaimed documentary bout the life of a death row inmate at 16 from the streets of DC. The student's name was Kevin Bruno and I couldn't wait to get up there and meet him and the rest of her students.

I hadn't been to DC since I was little. I usta go up there wit my moms and I just remember DC havin a lotta tall building and blacks folks everywhere and I remember my auntie livin right down the street from the White House. That always tripped me out, how close the hood was to the White house. I got there and did my presentation. At first some of them had that look on their face like "who is this nigga what the fuck he talkin bout?" Then as I kept goin they really started gettin into it, interruptin me askin me questions, they loved it, they told me they could relate to what I was tellin them bout life and they wished more people like me would come talk to them.

That shit made me feel hella good. It definitely was what I needed at the time. It was good for us all, feel me? I promised to stay in touch wit the lil homeys and as I rode the Greyhound back to North Carolina it felt as though my soul had been cleansed. The darkness of my grandmother's death was lightenin up.

CHAPTER 25

When I got back one day I was up at the BP sellin CD's and met this dude.

"What's up brotha you need some CD's?"

"What you got? You got your own original music?"

"Well I got that and anything else you need."

"Let me get your shit. Can I listen to it first?"

"No problem it might melt your dash board though, it's that hot. Fo real."

"Is that right?"

"Fo sho' cuz'n."

"Where you from homey?"

"I'm from the Bay. Northern California but I grew up down here too."

"You say this shit hot right?"

"Yeah hold up I'll be right back. Go ahead bump my shit. I got one of my regulars over here." I trotted over to a guy's car who always shopped wit me. I wasn't there two minutes when I heard a horn honkin loud as hell.

"Yo homey! Come 'mere homey," It was the dude listenin to my music.

I finished my business and walked over to the dude's car.

"Homey this you on this CD?"

"Yeah so what you think man?"

"I ain't gonna front, this is hot as fuck! Who y'all signed to?"

"We independent. I push our shit. feel me?"

"Look my name is ICM. I'm from New York and I represent Straight Face Records. My brother is the CEO and I'm down here in North Carolina scouting for southern acts. Right now we got an R&B singer Lumidee. She's doin pretty good in nationwide rotation. I personally would like to manage y'all."

"Is that right? Who you done managed before?"

"Well I did some work wit Bad Boy and Arista on a A&R level last year."

"I tell ya what, let me holla at my peoples and I'll get back at ya."

"Cool this my number. Can I keep the CD?"

"Yeah for $5 it's yours."

"Here you go Fleetwood I'll be lookin for your call."

I made a few calls to get some advice on the situation.

"Hello."

"Bub this Fleetwood."

"What up Fleet?"

"Say I met this dude ICM, says his brotha own Straight Face in New York wit a R&B singer out that's on Universal. He wanna manage us."

"Do he want y'all to sign a contract?"

"He didn't mention one yet. I don't know."

"What you say his name is and what's his brotha's label?"

"ICM and his brotha's label is Straight Face."

"Keep your phone on I'll call you right back."

After like forty-five minutes the phone rang.

"Fleet?"

"Yeah."

"Gone fuck wit him if you really think he believe in you and your music, but don't sign nothin till you talk to me. And have him manage what comes through your company not just you. That way you can work a better agreement."

"Most definitely Bub. Thanks."

"You know we family Fleet. Call me if you need me and don't sign shit without counsel hear me?"

"Yes sir, most definitely." The phone went dead and I called ICM. "Hello."

"Yo man this Fleetwood we'd like to sign wit you but also I'd like you to sign everyone that comes through my label, Block Money, wit a percentage comin to me."

"I think we can do business Mr. Fleetwood."

It wasn't a week and he had set us up wit a couple of shows and we rocked both of them. The next week he went to New York and took our music wit him. I still had my own connects so I wasn't trippin plus we didn't have no contract. When he came back he was real excited."

"Hello."

"Can I speak to Fleetwood?'

"Yeah this him who this?"

"This ICM what's up wit'cha Fleet?"

"Oh I'm chillin fam what's the business?"

"I got some good news for y'all"

"Yeah what's that?"

"Them people up top in New York loved y'all music. I got y'all set up for a showcase wit Ruff Ryder and Universal."

"You bullshittin man, when?"

"Next week. Can y'all make it?"

"Hell yeah!"

"I told you Fleet, I was gonna take you to the next level. Just give me a little time and watch what happen."

"Fo sho' my nigga. Fo sho'."

I was happy as fuck, like "bout fuckin time we finally bout to get on." I called Black.

"Yo what up Fleet."

"Black, dude got us a showcase in New York my nigga."

"When we leavin?"

"Next week."

"I'm ready Fleet. Shit I'm ready!"

"I'mma holla at ya my nigga. Be safe in them streets you gotta play it real smooth. You feel me?"

"I got'cha Fleet I gotcha"

It was close to Christmas 2003 and finally the day came to leave I was happy as fuck as we rode up the New Jersey turnpike. We were five deep in ICM's Exhibition: Lil Black, his homey Biz Money, Kareem, this young cat from Philly ICM was fuckin wit, and me. All I could think was "I ain't comin back without a contract. I aint comin home without a contract. When we arrived in New York we went straight into Bed Stuy on Nordstrom and Atlantic, dead smack in Biggie's old hood. The company was called Hatlantic Entertainment and it was owned by these Jamaican dudes. When we went up in the building I didn't really know what to expect. I was just glad to be there. We went up and there was an office building in the back. This sista greeted us.

"Hello my name is Kimonte. I heard you fella's music. I really was impressed."

"Thank you."

"What's your name"

'They call me Lil Black."

"And you?"

"Biz Money."

"And you must be Fleetwood?"

"Fo sho'."

"Well make yourselves comfortable. Is it anything I can get for you?"

"What time we perform" I asked. " We'd like to change and shit feel me?"

"Oh from what I understand you'll have more than enough time so you can just kick back and relax."

"Can we get something to drink maybe?"

"No problem." She walked out and was back hella fast.

"Here you go."

"Thanks."

"Thank you."

"Thank you."

"Not only are you dope but you have manners, that's very rare. It's gonna take you a long way in this game. Well, if you need anything just holla. I'm in the other room."

I looked and on the wall were a gang of Reggae posters. We kicked back for a minute then the studio engineer walked in.

"What's goin on Fellas? I'm Messiah. ICM has told us a lotta good thangs bout y'all."

"Hey what's up Messiah? Fleetwood."

"They call me Lil Black."

"Biz Money."

"I must say I really am impressed wit y'all music It's different and it's hot."

"Thanks man we tryin hard to put it down" Lil black said.

"So you the engineer of the studio" I asked him.

"Yeah I push the buttons around here. I also produce."

"So do y'all mostly make reggae music here?"

"We do both. Whatever the situation calls for."

"So all those reggae artist posters on the wall been through here?"

"Oh yeah actually this was one of the first studios Notorious Big recorded in too."

"Fo Real?"

"Yeah in his song I'm Maxi at the dread spot he raps bout."

"Okay, Okay."

I always was a fan of Biggie. Even though him and Pac had their beef he always was my second or third favorite rapper. When Messiah finished tellin bout Biggie shoutin him out this light skinned Jamaican dude walks in.

"How you doin mon" he asked, reachin his hand out to me.

"I'm cool brotha."

"My name is Rice, mon. This is my shit man, my shit. Understand?"

"Fo sho."

"Me like your music. Me really do brethren."

"Thanks fam, we just tryin to get on."

He turned to Lil Black and Biz Money.

"Rice, mon, Rice."

"What's up man, Lil Black"

"What's up Biz Money."

"Biz, Black, Fleetwood, we got good Jamaican food for you. You hungry man?"

"Hell Yeah" we all said at the same time.

"Come, come let's eat."

He led us into another room and we sat down and ate. Rice had a thick Jamaican accent and was real cool, but you could just tell he was dangerous at the same time. After we ate we had like two hours before the showcase so we lounged around and went in and outta the studio just listenin to beats and shit. ICM had left to pick his brotha up so everyone was waitin for him to come back. Turned out it was a few groups comin to the audition and as time passed they started to come in.

Now I was gettin anxious but I knew whatever they had they couldn't fuck wit us. Lil Black and Biz were talkin to Kimonte in the other room. Kimonte was a sista who had just broken up wit a famous reggae star that was recording at Hatlantic a few months prior. Now she was under Rice's wing and she pretty much ran the studio. She was thick as hell, kinda crazy though. It was some other females that worked there too, two Jamaican women, that looked like they weren't feelin Kimonte. It wasn't my business but I could tell it was tension. I just wanted to perform and impress somebody wit some money so they could put our shit out.

It was two hustlas that worked at the studio: a Jamaican dude named Dog and this Puerto Rican cat name FU, for Fuck You. This dude was a true New Yorker but had been down south to North Carolina and had a brotha who still lived down there. We really connected wit

FU, plus this nigga was dope as hell. He was frustrated wit the rap game and that's all he kept tellin us "fuck the rap game."

After bout three hours passed people started wondering where ICM was wit this cat from Universal. The nigga wasn't even answering the phone. The showcase was supposed to be at 7 PM and it was now 9:30 wit a studio full of frustrated people. Finally in comes ICM upset and erratic and everybody was tryin to talk to him and it just seemed like he couldn't handle it. I realized then that this dude wasn't capable of managing us. But I knew I had to still impress his brotha. He was by himself just him but still it was a close plug to universal. That's how I looked at it.

Three groups did their thang then it was our turn. As soon as the music came on it was over! We were the only crunk group there so the impact of the sound in the room was phenomenal. After we finished ICM's brotha locked his eyes in on me as we were walkin past.

"Y'all dope partner, really different. I'mma be in touch wit y'all we gonna make some things happen."

"Cool, like what you talkin bout and when?" I was amped that he liked it.

"Well wait till after the holidays and I'll have my brotha bring you back up here and we'll sit down and work things out."

"That sound good to us" Lil Black said.

We exchanged handshakes and his brother left. I never even told him my name or asked him his. Later that night after things died down ICM went in the office wit Rice and Kimonte. After bout thirty minutes he came out.

"Listen Fleetwood, Black, Biz I need to talk to y'all."

"What's up" I asked.

"To be honest wit you this music shit – managing your group – is too much for me. I think y'all are extremely talented and I wouldn't want to hold y'all careers back."

"So what you sayin man" Lil Black asked him.

"Well Rice and Kimonte expressed an interest in your group and they would like to manage y'all. I'm still gonna plug y'all in wit my

brotha at his label but if y'all agree Hatlantic will handle the nego-
tiations."

"I'm sayin man, what's the problem" I said to him even though I
knew what it was. The pressure was gettin to him.

"I just feel like I can't take your group to the level y'all need to
be at."

"Fo sho'."

"Black what you think?"

"Whatever's gonna get us on Fleet."

"Biz you cool wit it?"

"Fleet, y'all brought me in. I'm wit y'all fam."

"Cool, I think it might work out. Let's look at the paperwork."

We thanked ICM and he left. Me and Black went in the office and
signed a management deal. I knew I shouldn't have did the shit. Bub
had told me to holla at him first before I sign anything, plus I had
no lawyer but I was like "fuck it if they fuck us." I had read enough
of it and I knew enough bout a contract to know that shit wasn't
for life. I was just ready to get out there honestly. I got caught up in
the moment, feel me? But after all the bullshit it turned out to be
void anyway because of some bad wording. They gave us some bread
and we were cool. We went out, gave Biz some money and everyone
seemed happy. We still had a performance for Ruff Ryder the next
night, so we just kicked it. Later that night we all went to a small
Jamaican club next door.

The next day Black and Biz went to Connecticut to Biz's grandmother house to visit and get clothes. I had a cousin up there so I
went and changed there. When we all got back everybody was ready
to go to the club to perform. They had a stretch Hummer limo and
everything so we all piled in and went to this club in Manhattan. I
can't remember the name but it was phat as hell. It had like two DJ's
wit turn tables suspended from chains in each corner and girls up in
cages dancing. The stage was hella big wit a drop picture behind it of
a microphone and the bar was in the middle of the floor in a circle
shape goin around and around. The shit really had me spinnin wit

it. As we walked up stairs they started the show off wit a freestyle battle then the groups started rockin. This black dude wit glasses walked up wit Kimonte.

"Fleet, Black, Biz, this is Alex from Ruff Ryder."

"How y'all fellas doin?"

"We cool" Black said.

"Well I'm here to see what y'all can do. If y'all can really move the crowd."

"Sir if you got a camera, tape recorder or whatever push record immediately when we touch the stage so you can capture a moment of musical magic."

"Is that right?"

"We can show ya better than we can tell ya."

"Well I definitely been hearing some good thangs. I'll see you fellas after the show."

A Ruff Ryder rep there to see us perform. He said he had heard some good thangs bout us. We were up next and as he walked away, for the first time I got nervous. I looked and Biz and Lil Black were on the couch laid back. Kimonte told us we were up and as we walked through the crowd I started to get pumped. By the time we hit the stage and our music came on I had that feelin. We were in rare form and they loved us. Once again we were the only crunk group in the house and with the energy we had, the crowd couldn't help but feel it. Me and Black were goin back and forth wit our rhymes on time, then Biz was ad libbin behind us. It was something to see. A show for real. The crowd was at the edge of the stage amazed and people were comin from the back as the songs continued to come from us. We finished and walked through the crowd gettin hugs and pounds. Finally I saw the Ruff Ryder rep and the brotha's eyes where lit up.

"We bout to be in business together and make a lotta money."

"That sound good to me" I told him.

"I love your music and stage presence. I got your management's number and I'll be in touch next week. We'll have a business meeting."

"Cool, be easy man. We lookin forward to ridin ruff"

I was hyped but still we weren't signed yet. That night we all went back to the studio, packed up and left for North Carolina. When we got home for a few days I didn't see Black, then I ran into him and it was a funny vibe. He was on the run now and still hustlin. All he was sayin was "I gotta get on. I gotta do me." When I tried to explain how we had to play thangs, he wasn't tryin to hear it. Bout a week later Kimonte call.

"Fleet, I need y'all back up top. I got y'all booked for a radio show."

"I'll be there. When you send the ticket call me I'm bout to go pack."

"Okay will do see ya when ya get here."

They were supposed to give us some more money for an apartment when we got back up there. Black said he couldn't make it but he and Biz would be there that weekend. So I went by myself to New York. When I get there the tension in the studio between the two Jamaican women and Kimonte was thick. They all wanted to be wit Rice, I side stepped it as much as possible but it let me know the professionalism I was dealin wit. Rice had woman problems. It was obvious and it was startin to fuck wit the business. I went on the radio station wit Kimonte and FU. It was a underground satellite station. I did my thang, played our songs and they were feelin us. As I was bout to leave this dude from Queens – Lord Rock – came in. I'd been playin his video down south.

"Say I remember you Fleetwood. We sent ya my new video."

"Yeah I remember playin it. I got it in rotation matter of fact."

"Thanks Fleet, really man. That exposure is helpin my sales out."

"No problem homey, no problem."

After that we did a hot freestyle together then I went back and hung around the studio for the next three or four days recording music. Every now and then I would take a break and walk around Brooklyn but mainly I stayed at that studio. When Black and Biz finally showed up they walked in and I felt a funny vibe again. After they got settled in we went in the office and talked. The agreement was that they would find us an apartment but as the days passed nothin happened. Black and Biz decided to go back. When I came back it was a beef bout the money. Biz wasn't happy wit his cut. I tried to explain that he was only our hype man and he had just got wit our group less than two weeks prior to us goin to New York. But him and Black were homeys and the separation was there. The next day I'm up at Bp sellin CD's and I get a call.

"Robert?"

"Yes who is this?"

"This is Ms. Richmond."

"Hi Ms. Richmond. How you doin" I asked smilin. I was glad to hear from her.

"Robert I got some bad news for you son. I'm sorry."

"Some bad news? What you talkin bout?" My eyes were dancing and my mind was racin.

"Robert your grandma died a few hours ago. Your grandfather just called me."

"Who? What you talkin bout she died? They just said she was doin alright in the hospital!"

"I know son. Something happened overnight, some complications of some kind."

"Of some kind? Why did my grandfather call you instead of me?"

"I don't know Robert. He's dealin wit a lot and he just asked me to call you."

"Okay thank you Ms. Richmond. Let me call him right quick though."

"Okay son don't do nothin crazy. If you need me call me."

"Yes ma'am."

Man this shit is crazy. I had just talked to my grandfather a few days ago and he said Big Mama was in the hospital but it wasn't nothin serious and now I get this fuckin call. So I dialed my grand-daddy.

"Big Daddy, this is Robert, what happened to Big Mama? I thought you said it wasn't serious?"

"Son calm down, calm down. We don't know what happened. One day she was okay, the next night it was complications."

"How did they say how she died?"

"Heart failure son. Heart failure."

"Damn I just lost one grandmother. I don't believe this shit" I said, my voice crackin, tears runnin down my face.

"Big Daddy I'm on my way to Oakland."

"See ya when you get here son."

"Yes sir."

Three days later I'm sittin on a plane headed back to the bay. Fuckd in the head for real now. The group I put together seemed to be comin apart and I'd lost both of my grandmothers in the last 9 months. The only two unconditional love sources I had.

CHAPTER 26

I got to Oakland to my little sista's house and it was a strange feelin because my sista never got along wit my grandmother.

As the cab pulled off and I walked up the stairs I thought bout the times when I was little and Big Mama would talk to me bout words and the importance of knowledge and the difference of knowledge and wisdom. She taught me how to play Scrabble at age 5.

I had to share my other grandmother wit like 40 cousins but in Cali I only had to share Big Mama wit my sista and I was the oldest. She would tell me I looked dead on like my father, her only son and best friend. Big mama was my heart. She taught me so much and didn't judge what I did, just told me it came wit consequences. She allowed me to bump my head and hoped eventually it would start hurtin. When I finally went to see my grandfather he just sat in the chair. No emotion whatsoever.

After the funeral I went back to my little sista's house, changed clothes and went to San Francisco. It felt good to be back in my old stompin grounds even though a lotta my homeys was dead, in jail or strung out. Just to see the same block were I got my name and held my first sac. In a strange way it was refreshin cause people was givin me the look like "damn you still alive nigga?" It gave me the feelin that if I made it through this shit couldn't nothin stop me. One look around and it was obvious to me that nothin really had changed but the faces. It still was ho's, dope fiends, cops and killas everywhere.

I knew this female name Pam Pam who had a local access show like mine so I went and appeared on her show and her homey King Levell's show that same night. Two days later I was on my way back to North Carolina.

When I got home I got in touch wit Hatlantic and they wanted me to come back up there. When I got there it wasn't two days before shit hit the fan. The girls that worked there got fired because of the friction wit Kimonte. I told Rice I didn't want her guiding my career but I would fuck wit him. And that's when the shit came out.

She attacked me, sayin Lil Black and Biz didn't want to be down wit me and that they were goin solo. The cat was outta the bag now. Come to find out Kimonte had takin a likin to Biz and had been convincin him that me and Black had held out on the money. Biz was his boy so Black threw it off on me. After I analyzed it I knew what it was. Black's time was runnin out. He knew he was on his way to jail and he was tryin to grab hold to whatever he could. This broad Kimonte was tryin to get in anyway she could too.

She had slid under Rice, got two girls fired, but wit' a little knowledge of the game I had exposed the fact that she really didn't know what she was doin. Really I was still managing us when we were there. She was doin what I told her we needed done. She had never managed a group before. She was just around the underground LA scene wit some rap groups but hadn't really never did shit to get nobody on. I figured that out after we signed wit them but was like "fuck it, I'mma see what'll happen." Rice decided it was best for me to go back down south to let things blow over and when I got there he would Western Union the rest of the money. But when I got back all was waitin on me was trouble.

I had an interview wit Cee-lo and Trillville comin up so I tried to concentrate on that. Then one day I got a message from Rap-A-Lot Records invitin me to come and kick it wit them at the Super Bowl. I hadn't seen Black but Biz called.

"Fleet what up this Biz money."

"What up wit 'cha?"

"Fleet man y'all shitted on me in New York wit that money."

"How you figure that? You know you just got wit us two weeks ago. Do you know how much money I've invested into this group? Let alone you only got on 2 songs and only 1 is on the new project."

"So what? Y'all said I was part of the group so I should get an equal share."

"Ask Lil Black. When we was in the office negotiating. He the one said you didn't really deserve an equal share."

"What? You bullshittin."

"Nigga I'm tellin you the truth. That's your homeboy, ask him."

"You seen him Fleet?"

"N'all. Not at all."

"Man I don't believe he'd do me like that. You call the shots anyway he don't."

"Man no matter what I say you ain't gonna believe me. I got other shit to do. I'm gone."

I hung up and within two minutes the phone rang again. I wasn't bout to answer then I looked at the number and noticed the New York area code.

"Fleetwood, mon. This is Rice, mon."

"Oh what up Rice, how you doin?"

"Cool brethren, cool" he said in his thick Jamaican accent.

"So what's the business though?"

"Your money is in the Western Union mon. I did my part."

"Thanks Rice fo stickin to your word."

"Yeah I told'cha brethren. You seen Black?"

"N'all not really Rice."

"What's goin on Fleet?"

"Man the shit gonna work out hopefully. That's all I can say. Shit hopefully will work out."

"Yeah man, I invested my money into y'all."

"Look. Regardless, I only speak for myself, but I'm wit'cha Rice.

I'm wit'cha."

"Okay Fleet. Call me later man."

I hung up and got a ride to the closest Western Union. I got the money, gave Black his share but didn't give Biz shit. He didn't have nothin comin and after he calmed down he realized the same thang. But by now Black was really buggin out on some "fuck all y'all niggaz and Rice" type shit. The cat was like my little brotha and I had love for him but right at that moment I had to look out for me. I knew what it was that was gettin at him, he was a good nigga but facin prison was drivin the lil nigga crazy. I knew he was headed for a fall: toting pistols, stayin high all the time, and mad at the world wasn't a good combination, feel me? He had just got caught up again but somehow he got outta jail wit a warrant. He was one lucky muthafuckin cat.

This was around the time me and my auntie started havin problems. I wouldn't even come home. I started hangin out at another studio called Payroll, helpin out and writin hooks. I ended up doin the interview wit Cee-lo and Trillville right when they where blowin up. It was my last interview. After that I pretty much canceled the show and was "like fuck this shit."

One day I came to the studio to do a song wit Wonda but the singer I had didn't feel the hook. It was this dude name Rico there wit Wonda.

"Say Rico this is my homey Fleetwood. He got a hot hook he want you to sing on" Wonda told him.

"Oh what up Fleet, let me hear how the hook go."

I sung the hook the best I could.

"Damn that's hot yeah I can definitely do something wit that"

"Cool you ready now? I got the beat and everything is up."

"Let's do it."

He did it and it was super hot. The emotion in his voice, this cat was the truth. You could hear the soul comin all outta him, he sounded like a young Teddy Pendergrass. We did like ten tracks just on his vocals. The song was called "Ancestors" and you can find it on my

"We Connected volume one" mixtape. Turned out he was Fantasia's brotha, the one on American Idol who was in the finals at the time. A few weeks passed and I was workin on a mixtape I was bout to drop. I had a lotta shit comin at me at the time so I started drinkin heavy and smokin hella weed which is never good. One night I got a call that Black was locked up and wasn't gettin out. I called New York.

"Can I speak to Rice?"

"Who is this?"

"Yo, this is Fleetwood man."

"Hold up Fleet. What up though? This is FU."

"What up FU?"

"Man shit done exploded up here. Rice got rid of that broad Kimonte and the studio been shut down for bout 3 weeks. It's hella slow around here."

"Damn fo real? So where Rice at?"

"He in the office, hold on. I'mma go get him."

"Hello Fleetwood man. What happenin?"

"Man shit crazy. Lil Black's in jail. I'm still holdin shit down though."

"Well man let's just take a break and let things die down. In a couple of months we'll crank it back up."

"Whatever you think is best, just remember I'm wit'cha Rice."

"Yeah Fleet I know that. I know that."

Just that fast thangs were crumblin. I didn't really trip, they were still playin my song on the radio and I had a cat at Priority/Capitol that had told me he would fuck wit me. Plus I still had LiL FLIP number and was still waitin on the the Youngbloods to come off tour so i wasn't trippin.

One day this balla nigga came to the studio from Atlanta. The whole time I was just tellin stories as usual, being me. I never looked at it like I was tryin to be funny, but this dude thought I was hilarious.

"Say bro what's your name" he asked.

"They call me Fleetwood partna."

"You got to be one of the funniest niggaz I ever seen or heard in my life."

"Is that right?"

"Man I just paid a nigga $2500 for 15 minutes and the crowd just looked at his azz. Shit I been in this room 20 minutes and all you been doin is talkin and all these niggaz been doin is laughin. You a funny muthafucka man. You ever thought bout being a comedian?"

"N'all I ain't no comedian homey. I rap, produce, write hooks. I just been blessed wit the ability of wordplay and got a gang of stories that's all."

"That's what I mean. You just described what a comedian is. A nigga wit stories and wordplay. Look I don't know too much bout that rap shit but I got the south locked on this comedy scene. Here's my card. You come to Atlanta and I'll make you a star, I guarantee you that."

From what I could tell this nigga had paper so I took his card.

"Yo homey I should be comin down there soon to fuck wit the the Youngbloods' producer. Mark Twain."

"Mark Twain? I'll take you to his house, I know that nigga. Just when you get there make sure you call me."

"Fo sho' and thanks cuz'n."

It was later that night that me and D.J. Coyote got into an argument over a show that I wasn't included in. This dude kept sayin how we was family ridin together on this music shit and all but when it came down to it he wasn't tryin to let me do my thang wit his group and knew I could rock a show. He had seen it. I think it was because he knew I would out shine them easy. They had arranged to do a show at my cousins club and never asked me to get on the ticket, so I felted disrespected. I called him and told him. He said some ol square shit and I hung up. I was mad, like "fuck them then. I don't need them on my project."

"Say Nyborn erase all them niggaz shit off my project. I don't want that shit on there."

"Fleet when you say fuck Coyote you includin me. I'm on his label" Wonda told me later.

"Take it anyway you want it homey. This Block Money Music (that was the name of my label at the time before "Boyz n the hood" came out) my nigga on mines fo life. I gives a fuck bout anything else fo real."

"Fleet man why don't you holla at Coyote" Wonda asked me.

"Ain't shit to say my nigga. I said what I had to say feel me?"

This was fucked up cause DJ Coyote and I where cool until we tried to do business together. That evening my auntie called the studio.

"Hello?"

"Robert this is Aunt Barbara. You need to come and get your belongings outta my house. I can't allow you to live here any longer."

"What's all this bout?"

"Some girl just came over here ringing my doorbell talkin crazy bout you and her where supposed to be in the drug business together and you had her money. Then the police came after that. It's just too much for me Robert."

"Aunt Barbara she lyin. You believe that? Come on now? I ain't got nowhere to go though."

"That's not my problem."

"Okay Okay. I'll be over there to get my stuff tonight."

I hung up. Fuck, what else could go wrong? I went and got my shit and went back to the studio and Nyborn let me crash there. Two weeks had passed and me and Rico and his brotha Joe had got kinda tight but D.J. Coyote was screamin Fantasia hard on the radio so it was tension there. One night we was in the studio wit some strippers and one of them over stepped her bounds.

I was talkin to Panama Black and my homey I.Q. the Hustla.

"Q do you know what? I should go shut them niggaz' show down."

"I don't like them niggaz no way" Panama said.

"Fleet you know I'm wit'cha my nigga." I.Q. said.

"That's some ho azz shit Fleetwood." One of the strippers said outta no where.

" First of all who the fuck is you? I don't even know you. You need to stay in a ho's place and out a gangster's conversation or do what you do best. Take your clothes off like the tramp you is. Bend over and pick this dollar up ." I reached in my pocket and threw a dollar on the floor.

"Damn Fleet why you talkin to her like that" Nyborn asked.

"Man quit savin these ol nasty azz ho's my nigga."

"Fleetwood I'm sorry" the stripper apologized.

"That's the first smart thang you said . You sorry. Cause you a sorry excuse for what a woman suppose to be. Next time you speak to a gangsta you better check his homework first tramp."

"Okay Fleetwood that's it man the girl said she was sorry you need to get your shit and leave."

"Man you gonna front on me behind these tramps? Fuck you then."

I got all my shit and IQ gave me a ride to my other auntie Bobbie Ireland's house where I had moved into.

The next day I'm on a bus headed for Atlanta. I had a cousin down there. When I got there he came to get me and I got settled in and called Greg. The nigga said he wanted me to be a comedian.

"What's up homey this Fleetwood. I'm in ATL."

"Oh what's up Fleet how you doin?"

"I'm cool just ready to make something happen."

"Look I'm outta town right now I'll be back in a week. Lay low and when I get back we gonna work."

"Fo sho."

I waited but the whole time I never stopped drinking and smokin weed which didn't help at all. Every now and then I would hit the block but basically I stayed in the house waitin to hear from this cat. By the time he called me I was hella frustrated.

"Hello."

"Speak to Fleetwood?"

"This him."

"Fleet what up homey this Greg."

"Yeah what's up man."

"Look I'mma set something up for ya in a few days I just got back in the A."

"Man look to be honest wit you I ain't no damn comedian. Fuck that comedy shit. I ain't the funny part of a nigga joke, real talk." I hung up in his face then took the phone off the hook.

That night I was on a Greyhound back to Cali. I had called my cousin Terry and he was like "just go back to Cali." Ridin that Greyhound thinkin bout all that had happened – my grandmothers dyin, the shit that happened in New York, I'd just left the TV show. Shit was all bad.

I felt like hip hop was tryin to kill me.

I had spent the last 15 years fuckin wit this rap game and the closer I got it seemed like the further I was gettin from being happy. So my attitude towards rap was like fuck it. Right when I got in town I ran into Bizzy Ben.

"What's up? What you been up to? You still fuck wit the music" the first thang he said.

I wasn't really into the mood to explain all the shit that had just went down, in the back of my mind I wanted my homey to be like "is that you on there" when he heard my shit. So I let him hear my song called "That's Whats Up."

"You know Messy got a song called "That's What's Up" too Fleetwood. They playin the shit outta it all on the radio."

"You bullshittin Ben."

"Fo real my nigga."

I couldn't believe that shit. That's when I told myself "man fuck this rap shit." I had counted on comin to the west, lettin my single bubble and keep things goin, but now this shit. I realized then that pursuin this music was killin me. I had to take a break.

I got settled in and for like a year I didn't do shit in the music game. I just worked, stayed out the way and got me somewhere to stay. Fantasia won American Idol and I seen Rico on TV singin backup. I was happy for him. I also heard that DJ Coyote and them were doin there thing. I usta see people in the city and they would ask me bout my music sayin "Fleet you need to go ahead and put that shit out." I appreciated it but I was cool. This was the first time in my life in 15 years I was away from the business. One day I ran into Kevin Epps.

"I gotta office downtown homey. Why don't you come through and kick it wit ya boy sometime."

"Cool Kev I really appreciate that cuz'n. I'mma do that."

"Fleet don't be bullshittin my nigga make sure you come."

"Kev I'mma be there."

The next day I was there and he was workin on "Rap Dreams" starring Mistah FAB, Hectic, and Kev Kelley. He was workin on a documentary called the "Black Rock" bout the plight of the black prisoners on Alcatraz. I hung out wit him every chance I could. It was cool to kinda be around the shit again but the fire was gone. I had no desire to touch the mic.

Then one day I ran into my old school homey from the TL, Tony Coleman. He told me he had his own studio and he knew I was in the music business prior so he invited me in.

"Tone I really ain't tryin to fuck wit that music shit no more homey. I'm done, I had my run. Got a little change and a little fame. The shit took me through so much turmoil. It damn near destroyed me."

"Are you happy right now" he asked.

"I'm cool. Shit could always be worse, you feel me?"

"Yeah but wood you ain't happy. You ain't at peace. You know why?"

"Why is that?"

"Because you ain't doin what God blessed you to do."

"And what's that homey?"

"Make music to inspire people. I heard your shit back in the day. See, some niggaz make music Fleetwood, but you make history."

"Thanks man, but that shit drove a nigga crazy."

"That's because your spirit was broken. It was a hole in your soul. You're a very spiritual individual Fleet. So your spirit got to be right for anything else in your life to be right. You understand what I'm sayin?"

"Fo sho' homey. I been really thinkin bout goin back to church, shakin this weed and all this drinkin too."

"Just pray my nigga. Whatever you do, keep prayin."

One night I came to his studio and his whole crew came to the lab. He introduced me and then put me on the spot. He put on a beat and he was like Fleet write something to this. The track was hot and I was feelin it so I grabbed a pen and paper and started writin. I had 16 bars in like 15 minutes. I don't know it just flowed. I walked in the booth last and smashed it. Tone said the shit was hot but I felt it was alright. I felt something walkin out that booth though.

The fire was burning again.

The reason I titled this book "Hip Hop tried 2 Kill Me" was because it was all I loved. It was my life focus. I put all my eggs in that one basket and that's never good. When you love something that much other things in your life will get neglected. I loved rap so much I forgot bout myself. Now I understand hip hop and appreciate it. Momma always told me what don't kill you will make you stronger and it did it make me stronger. It took me to places I never thought I'd go and brought things outta me that I never thought I possessed.

It killed that person I was at the time, but also gave birth to the person I am today – an individual who has morals and values that won't be compromised for nothin and the ability and desire to shed some light on the youth of this generation bout the struggling side of hip hop.

I only see success in front of me cause GOD is guiding me I know it'll be a few potholes waiting for me to step in and I probably will, but I'mma keep on keepin on believe that, like the Curtis Mayfield song playa, cause it ain't about how many times you fall it's all about how many times you get up. As you can see Hip Hop didn't kill me it just gave me a story.

To all my loved ones, whatever you do put God first and what you want won't be far behind. Real talk.

This that west coast country boy himself your kinfolks
– Fleetwood Peace

EPILOGUE

I must say I'm hella happy bout my book being completed. If you reading this then that means you got it so that's a good thang, feel me?

My goal in life is to show God how much I love him and thank him by doin what's right. I try hard but I'm not perfect, far from that. That's why I pray every mornin. I know I could easily be in a prison somewhere or in a grave or strung out on dope, feel me?

Everyday I try to be an inspiration to people and let God use me as a tool for change. I love Hip Hop because it's my gift to get to the little homeys. It's our common ground. They feel my pain, hear my stories and see my progress in life through my music. I share my choices wit them in the studio. Hip Hop has allowed me to reinvent myself so many times. It's given me a legacy that no one can erase or take away and it helped me make history. That's why I love it so much and always will.

With that in mind these are the things that have been keepin me busy in the community.

Right now I'm sitting in the Lab waiting on my lil Homey Jermaine aka Whop. A real hot young beat maker and rapper from the Bay Area. We working on a project together – "The West Coast Country Boy" it's coming together real good. You know I definitely feel blessed. I could be alotta other places on a Friday nite I just got a call before I came, they want me back up in Portland next month to do a show with CBO and KILLA TAY so that's got me pumped. I just left there like three weeks ago rocking the Living Legends Tour with RBL POSSE, SPICE 1, and CELLY CEL and you know I did my thang, real talk. To be honest I've rocked alotta shows but this was special. It had been awhile since my last show and for me to be on stage with some cats that I really admire, grew up listening to, and to hold my own, that was really special for me feel me. Next week I'll be starting writing my next book, I'm really looking forward to that. After whop leaves tonight I got a interview on my homey T-Kash show KPFA. He always show me love his show is going nationwide tonite so that's big and he invited me on there you feel me, life is Good homey.

Tone ask me to be a part of the production team and we began puttin together his project, "One Fam Radio." It's finished now and it's hot. It should be on the streets summer 2007. I also hooked up wit my partna Bizzy Ben again who runs a non-profit community organization called Straight Forward Club. It works wit inner city youth and young adults in San Francisco teaching boxing, hip-hop and entertainment wit a therapeutic twist.

Bizzy Ben launched a hip-hop movement called One Block Move-ment that works to bring the hip hop community together one block at a time. Using hip hop as a vehicle, we go to juvenile hall and holler at the little homeys.

I developed my own situation for change in the community called the "Homeboy Hotline". What I do is provide job leads and resources for ex-offenders upon their release helpin them wit there re-entry into the community. I'm tryin hard to get the homeys off the block and keep them outta those cages, feel me? And I'm very proud to say that I started writin columns for The Oakland Post newspaper and also The Bayview in San Francisco, something I never dreamed of. I also joined an organization wit Tone called "All of Us Or None." It's made up of formerly incarcerated people who fight against laws and policies that affect people wit criminal records. We just got the question askin you bout your criminal past taken off of city job applications in San Francisco.

I'm workin very closely wit Rudy Corpuz, founder and director of the United Playa's – an organization that's been makin a powerful impact for change in the Bay area for the last 15 years wit the youth. Rudy is a good brotha and dear friend of mine. He was the one who set it up where I could go to San Quentin Prison during Black History Month 2006 to do a concert, two weeks after Tookie Williams got killed.

While touring San Quentin I ran into Harry O. We keep in contact and he works wit the United Playas to help make a change in the community and also he supports my homeboy hotline. We stay in contact and he's waitin on an appeal to come through. I just try to tell the homey to stay close to God and he does, real talk.

I've released a series of mixtapes entitled "We connected" Vol. 1/2/3 and I'm workin on volume 4 as I write this. The purpose of these mixtapes is to give exposure to the up and comin hip hop artists around the nation and at the same time, form a network and database of resources, video shows, retail stores, radio stations in each city.

So far I've connected wit North and South Carolina, Virginia Beach, VA, Minneapolis, St. Paul, MN, Baton Rouge, Los Angeles, Queensbridge, Las Vegas, New York, Washington, D.C, Portland, Utah, New Mexico, Texas, Alabama and of course the Bay is all on the projects. Hopefully by the time Vol. 5 comes out I'll have half the US on one mixtape.

I released an EP entitled "Hot Mess" wit four new joints. You can find it on my www.myspace.com/Fleetwood189. Also I got the compilation "We Connected Vol. 1" comin soon wit Messy Marv, San Quinn, Yin Yang Twins, JT the Bigga Figga and many more. I'm just basically gettin my name in circulation again. I'm puttin myself in the position to be one of the most powerful ghost writers in the industry, trust me.

The "We Connected" volumes will continue to come out and by

the time this book comes out the soundtrack to my book will also be on the streets, I got like forty songs already in the safe and I have a project entitled the DOPE BOYZ (Doin. Our. Part. Equally.) It's my way of thankin GOD musically. The mixtape is finished and the album will be out by early fall.

THE DOPE BOYZ, remember that name.

As I write this I have my next book "Blood test" in the works. It's half way done so I'm just tryin to stay busy feel me.

I still fuck wit Bub. He always believed in me and he reassured me that he had my back. Told me to stay at my shit. So that's what I been doin. Man I'm still at this shit. Trust me after all the bull shit and I'm still here. I think GOD took my gift from me because I didn't appreciate it.

I let the youth know bout the importance of ownin your own masters because if you ain't got the masters you a slave. I explain to them how important it is to stay independent and get a distribution deal where you get 85% of the royalties off a record instead of signin a record deal and get 15% of your royalties. The bay area right now is back wit the hyphy movement. Artists gettin signed but they also signin the homey's companies to distribution deals. We out in Oakland and we learned early from Too $hort: fuck the radio and fuck being on TV. Go in the studio make you an album. Sell 10,000 at $7 dollars a piece through a local distributor and that's $70,000 a decent livin for a year. But now when you put out 3 albums a year that's 210,000. That's ballin independently.

That's what we do in the Bay and that's what we encourage people to do. Don't concentrate on being on MTV or BET cause everybody you see on TV ain't got no money. The record companies rent certain props to keep up an image for the artist When In all reality after the advances and everything is paid for that took them to make your record usually you end up with nothing. Now take Into account the computer age the music business changes everyday. It can be extremely devastating to find out someone has took all your creativity and they are the ones eating off It This is the reason you find a lot of former and current artist with drug and drinking problems in the industry. See without a strong spiritual foundation you'll never last in the entertainment business because it's full of devils – immoral and unethical people who don't value God but idolize money and makin a profit.

Anybody you see in the entertainment business who has been successful for a long period of time and who ain't strung out on some drugs or a drunk has God deeply in their life, believe that homey. They talk crazy bout Will smith but he pimped the whole game. Study him and Ice Cube.

What I try to get people to remember is the devil was the chief musician in heaven so music is a sure fire way he uses to destroy one's soul. You got to stay close to God dealin wit this devilish business of music. Usually by the time most artists realize they're gettin fucked for their talents and creatively they're at the point where they can circulate at all the celebrity parties and drown their sorrows in booze and drugs. After bout 10 of them parties and 4 or 5 conversations wit your peoples bout why you ain't got shit, the depression kicks in. For most it's devastatin. They never find their way back and I'm happy to say the rest turn to the only source left, God. That's why you see so many former artists into gospel includin me. We just get tired of all the devilment. Make no mistake I'm still a gangsta though, a true soulja. But today I'm one of God's souljas, fightin for righteousness because I know I'll always be a sinner. That's why I will always pray.

As you can see it's far from over for me. I just wrote my first book of many more are to come.

For more information about my up and coming projects please go to www.myspace.com/Fleetwood189.

NOTE FROM THE AUTHOR

To every one of you reading this, i cannot thank you enough for being avid supporters of my work. You all allowed me to make one of my dreams a reality. Because you gave me the strength to wanna write something great that could describe why i love hip hop. This is the first of many of my stories to come, I truly appreciate you taking the time to let my world enter yours.

In closing i would like to say that hip hop is a billion dollar industry, homey get yours out of it. Don't be the saddest sight ever seen, that's "wasted talent, don't be no one's hooker for some rims, scaper and some good weed and your family still be In the hood starving feel me. Be Independent be a real CEO don't just have a logo on a chain really be a label, cause it's all about business.

MAY GOD BLESS ALL YOUR ENDEAVORS

PLEASE REST N PEACE HOMEYS

MARVIN EASTER – NORTHDSIDE, MN
CAPONE – MEMPHIS, TN
TREYMAINE BROWN – FILLMORE, CA
WARREN CRAWFORD – MOUNT ZION, NC
ERIC SLAUGHTER – NORTHSIDE MINNEAPOLIS, MN
WALTER "STUFF" LITTLE JR
LIL BOOTSIE – GREENSBORO, NC
PETE BROWN – GREENSBORO, NC
STEVE HARLEY – GREENSBORO, NC
KENNETH TATE – GREENSBORO, NC
KENNY BAILEY – GREENSBORO, NC
MIKE BARTLEY – GREENSBORO, NC
CASSANDRA SHELTON – GREENSBORO, NC
RODNEY LEWIS – HUNTERS POINT, CA
NAPPY (WOO block GENERAL) – HUNTERS POINT, CA
RONDO – PAGE ST, CA
RAMBO – PAGE ST, CA
ARONDO DAVIS – MINNEAPOLIS, MN
REGGIE MILEY – WASHINGTON, DC
CHUCK – HUNTERS POINT, CA
BIG BEN HUNTERS POINT, CA
HAMP "MONEY BAGS" BANKS JR.
CHAUNCEY BAILEY JR.

IT'S A DAMN SHAME BUT I COULD HAVE EASILY FILLED THIS
PAGE UP WITH SO MANY NAMES OF VICTIMS OF VIOLENCE IN
THE URBAN COMMUNITY. PLEASE LET'S STOP KILLING EACH
OTHER HOMEY AND FOR THE ONES NOT ON HERE, I DIDN'T
FORGET YOU, AND YOU'LL NEVER BE FORGOTTEN.

MAY GOD BLESS YOUR SOULS

coming soon

Blood
test

by

Fleetwood

Including Soundtrack

FLEETWOOD's had a long journey trying to find the treasures in Hip Hop and, in his days, became a writer, rap artist, music producer, actor, videographer, motivational speaker and community activist.

He has an Associate Arts Degree in Music Engineering from Music Tech in Minneapolis.

This is Fleetwood's first book. To find out more about Fleetwood, his next book, his community acitivism and to listen to his music, go to myspace/fleetwood189.

COLOPHON

Chaparral® | Designer: Carol Twombly

Created by Adobe® type designer Carol Twombly, Chaparral combines the legibility of slab serif designs popularized in the 19th century with the grace of 16th-century roman book lettering. Like the drought-resistant brush that blooms on the arid coastal range near Twombly's California home, Chaparral's highly functional design is surprisingly beautiful.